SNOWBOUND
for
CHRISTMAS

*Love Blankets a Pair
of Inspirational Novellas*

D1466646

ANDREA BOESHAAR

DEBBY MAYNE

Published by Barbour Publishing, Inc., P.O. Box 719, Uhrichsville, Ohio
44683, www.barbourbooks.com

Our mission is to publish and distribute inspirational products offering excep-
tional value and biblical encouragement to the masses.

Member of the
Evangelical Christian
Publishers Association

Printed in the United States of America.
5 4 3 2 1

SNOWBOUND
for
CHRISTMAS

LET IT SNOW!

by Andrea Boeshaar

Dedication

This story is dedicated to two of my favorite
missionaries who serve the Lord in Cambodia.
They don't run an orphanage
(like the one in this story), but they have
adopted two precious Cambodian children.
The missionaries to whom I refer
have hearts to see souls saved and have
dedicated their lives to The Great Commission.
For this reason, a percentage of royalties earned
from this novella will go to support their ministry.

Chapter 1

Oh, the weather outside is frightful, but the fire is so delightful. . . .

Sharon Rose Flannering leaned forward and turned off her car stereo. She always enjoyed singing along with the classic seasonal song, but the weather outside really was frightful tonight, and she had to concentrate on her driving.

The wipers flapped from right to left in a futile attempt to keep the windshield free of snow. Visibility was next to nil. Shari could see only a blur of white on the road before her.

"Lord, I know I said I missed snow on Christmas, but You didn't have to do exceeding, abundantly, above all I asked in this circumstance."

In spite of the situation, Shari chuckled. *A merry*

heart does good, like medicine. With everything she'd been through in the last ten years, she'd needed a heavy dose of merriment—that saving medicine referred to in Proverbs 17:22. God had proven Himself trustworthy throughout her life's many trials. His Word rang true. Besides, God's remedy cost nothing compared to psychotherapy and antidepressants. Most likely, those would have been her options had Shari not learned to chuckle in the face of adversity. Moreover, laughter kept the joy alive in her heart. She felt happy. Life was good. God was in control.

Even in the midst of a Wisconsin blizzard like this one.

Shari's cell phone rang, and she managed to flip it open and answer it with one hand without taking her eyes off the road as her car continued to creep along the interstate. "Hello?"

"Where are you?" Her mother's voice held a note of concern.

"I'm not sure. I can't see anything."

"Oh, no! And I don't even know what to tell you. We weren't supposed to get this storm until tomorrow."

Shari laughed. "I haven't been gone so long that I've forgotten Wisconsin's fickle weather."

"We should have all gone to Florida to see you this Christmas."

"We celebrate that way every year, Mom. And now, with Greg gone. . ."

Shari didn't finish the sentence. No need to. Her husband of twenty-three years had suffered with brain cancer for nearly a decade, and Shari's family had endured the emotional highs and lows of his illness right along with her. Surgeries and radiation treatments had kept Greg's disease in check for a while, but the time came when doctors could do no more. Since Greg knew Jesus Christ in a personal way, Shari couldn't feel sad that God chose to deliver her husband from his terrible pain and perform the ultimate healing—taking Greg to heaven. But she still mourned the loss of her husband, and this was her first Christmas without him. That was one of the reasons she had chosen to come home.

Home. Funny how Wisconsin still seemed like home, even though she'd lived elsewhere for more than half her life.

Suddenly, brake lights shone red through the swirling snow ahead, and Shari snapped back to attention. A moment later, she rejoiced. "Mom, a salt truck is right in front of me. Isn't that awesome? I'll follow this truck until I can figure out where I am, then I'll call you back."

"Please be careful, honey. I'm so worried about you. I just knew you shouldn't have driven all the way from Pensacola."

"I'm fine. Don't fret."

Shari quelled her impatience with her mother. Sylvia Kretlow was a pastor's wife, yet she couldn't come close to scraping up enough faith to equal that of the tiny mustard seed Jesus referred to in the Gospel of Matthew. She assumed the worst in all situations. Shari's dad, the minister, wasn't much better. He had a gloom-and-doom outlook on life, insisting he was "serious-minded." However, his somber attitude had caused him to keep a choke hold on Shari and her siblings during their teenage years, which only fueled their rebelliousness. If Shari hadn't run off with Greg Flannering at the age of twenty, she might never have come to trust Christ as her Savior. As it stood now, her sister and two brothers had yet to arrive at a saving knowledge of Him.

And that was another reason for her visit to Wisconsin. Shari hoped to be used as an instrument of God's love during this holiday season. Since Greg's death, Shari had never felt more determined to reach a lost and dying world with the Christmas story—and that included her siblings. Unfortunately, they'd had the salvation message hammered into their heads since birth. Words wouldn't reach them anymore. God would have to do something miraculous in order to reach Mark, Luke, and Abby.

"It seems like tragedies always happen during Christmastime," her mother lamented. "I don't want our family to suffer another loss this year. Greg's dying was hard enough."

Shari grinned. "Mom, your optimism is *so* encouraging."

Sylvia clucked her tongue at the quip.

"Let me figure out where I am," Shari repeated, "and then I'll call you back."

"All right, but please be careful."

"I will. I promise."

Shari disconnected the call and forced herself to relax. Following the enormous truck made driving a hundred times easier. However, ten miles later, the truck veered onto the exit ramp. Shari followed the truck, realizing too late that she'd left the interstate. Then, just to her right, she saw a well lit green and white sign advertising a Stop 'n' Shop. She pulled into the gas station/convenience store and decided this would be the perfect opportunity to determine her precise location.

Parking alongside a pump, grateful for the overhead protection from the storm, Shari filled her vehicle's gas tank before entering the store. The clerk couldn't have been more than nineteen. He was chatting with three scraggly young men who leaned on the counter, smoking cigarettes. They seemed harmless enough, although Shari wrinkled her nose at the noxious smell. She noticed the blue haze lingering over the counter-enclosed cashier area. To her relief, however, the rest of the store didn't seem smoky.

She visited the ladies' room then returned to the checkout counter just as a country-western rendition of "Silent Night" resounded through the speakers.

"So, I'm just now entering Green Bay?" Shari blinked in surprise at the clerk's response to her question. It seemed like an eternity had passed since she'd driven through Manitowoc. Under normal weather conditions, the drive between the two cities would have taken about thirty minutes.

"Where you headed?" the ruddy-faced young man asked.

"Forest Ridge. It's a little town in Door County just on the other side of the bay."

"I know where it is." He finger-combed his dark brown hair away from his forehead. "Wouldn't try to make it there tonight, though."

Shari frowned. "But it's Christmas Eve."

All four young men gave her sympathetic shrugs.

"There are a few hotels on the other side of I-43," a guy with a pockmarked face suggested before he blew a plume of smoke into the air. "You might want to stay at one of 'em."

"Yeah, snow's not s'posed to let up for a while," the clerk said.

Shari shook her head. "I want to be with my family. I've driven all the way up from Florida to spend the holidays with them."

"Should've arrived yesterday." The clerk grinned. "It was forty degrees outside."

Shari had thought the same thing a bazillion times while journeying through several long, uninteresting states; however, she hadn't been able to get off work any earlier. She'd considered flying, but the heightened terrorism alerts made Shari too nervous to board an aircraft.

Back in her car, she phoned her mother. After a few minutes, Shari's father got on the line.

"You're near Miriam Sheppard's bed-and-breakfast. She calls it a 'highway haven,' and it stays open all year long. Why don't you spend the night there?"

"With the Sheppards?" Shari let go with a peal of

laughter. "I don't think so."

"Why not? Miriam asks about you all the time. She's probably alone tonight. Your mother's nodding her head and. . . What? Oh, Karan's at her in-laws' and Brenan is in Africa. No, make that Brazil."

Shari knew Brenan's whereabouts already. Her church supported his mission team and she read their quarterly newsletter. Dr. Brenan Sheppard had come a long way from the quiet, lanky guy Shari dated in high school and two years into college. Back in those days, Brenan had about as much ambition as demonstrated by those young men inside the gas station. While Shari didn't regret breaking off their engagement, she was sorry for the way in which she did it—an unkind, impersonal letter.

Then, she ran off and eloped with Greg Flannering. At the time, Greg and his family were new to the area. Shari met Greg at an infamous, late-1970s disco. It was love at first sight for both of them, even though Shari was engaged to Brenan.

Years later, after she committed her life to Christ, Shari wrote Brenan a much different letter and apologized. He never replied, and she didn't try to contact him again. But she'd heard he never married, and she always felt responsible—like the woman who irreparably broke the poor man's heart. So, she prayed for him, asking God to bring a wife into Brenan's life. Still, staying at his mother's bed-and-breakfast seemed a little intimidating, even though Shari had always liked Miriam. The older woman was a widow, too. Her husband died years ago, and instead of moving back to Forest Ridge where she'd raised her children, Miriam continued to run the bed-and-breakfast, a small but profitable business that began after the older pair retired.

But it was sad that Miriam wouldn't have family around her tonight.

"She's alone, huh?"

"Shall I have your mother give Miriam a call?"

Gazing through her windshield, Shari felt as though she'd been planted inside a snow globe. At once, she saw the wisdom in not attempting the rest of the drive. "Yeah, go ahead. If worst comes to worst, I'll find a hotel."

"Okay, we'll call you right back."

Stepping out of her car again, Shari traipsed back into the Stop 'n' Shop. She purchased a cup of coffee and sat down at one of the four tables near the restrooms. As she sipped the too-strong brew, Shari felt glad she'd donned her comfy, wrinkle-free black knit dress and button-down red holiday sweater this morning. She had stayed overnight in Cincinnati and had felt determined to drive straight through to Forest Ridge today. She should have made it in ten or eleven hours, including lunch and bathroom stops. She had hoped to arrive in time for church, already dressed for the occasion.

Too bad the weather decided not to cooperate with her plans.

Shari's cell phone rang, and she answered it. "What took so long?"

"Oh, I'm sorry," her mother said. "Miriam and I got to chatting. Anyway, she said it's fine. She'd love to have you. She's got plenty of room in her bed-and-breakfast. It's right near the gas station where you are now."

Shari listened carefully to the directions. The Open Door Inn couldn't be more than a mile away.

"Great. I'm off. I'll call you after I get settled." She tamped down her disappointment over not seeing her family tonight. "Merry Christmas, Mom."

"Merry Christmas, honey. We'll see you tomorrow and celebrate then. At least I'll know you're safe tonight."

"Right. G'night."

Shari ended the call and shrugged back into her black wool coat. After wishing a Merry Christmas to the four young men still congregated around the checkout, she ventured back out into the winter wonderland.

"At forty-three years old, you're finally getting married." Karan Strang shook her head, and her honey-blond hair swished across her shoulders. "I can't believe it."

Brenan grinned, enjoying his sister's reaction to his news. "Well, I haven't popped the question yet. Elena could always turn me down."

Karan lowered herself onto the floral-upholstered settee. "Doesn't sound like she will."

Brenan didn't think so either. The dark-haired beauty he'd met in Brazil had gotten under his skin in the most unusual way. *It must be love.* Elena said she loved him. It's just that she was only thirty, and the difference in their ages bothered him a little.

Brenan glanced at the doorway in time to see his brother-in-law, Daniel Strang, enter the living room. Brenan's niece, Laura, and her husband, Ian, followed.

"Mom is stunned." Daniel combed strong fingers through his graying hair. "We pulled off our surprise without a hitch."

Karan grinned and lifted nine-month-old Chrissy onto her lap. Brenan still couldn't believe his sister was a grandmother. Or that he was a great-uncle. But seeing Chrissy, a picture of health, reminded him of the Cambodian orphanage he'd had on his mind for some time now. However, he shook off the burden. There wasn't anything he could do to help the missionaries in that part of the world. He'd been called to serve in Brazil. With Elena.

"And here Mom thought she'd spend Christmas Eve alone," Karan said, bouncing the baby on her knee. "Brenan, it was so cool that your plane got in before the bad weather hit."

"Amen to that!"

At that moment, Miriam Sheppard strode into the room carrying a tray of cookies. She looked happy, two rosy spots brightening her cheeks, and Brenan was glad he had made the effort to come home for the holidays.

"We're going to have another guest." Setting the decorated treats on the table, Miriam straightened. She looked at Brenan. "You'll never guess who's coming."

"Who?"

"Shari Kretlow. Of course, her last name isn't Kretlow anymore. But for the life of me, I can't think of what it is."

"Flannering." Brenan hadn't forgotten it. Where he once had rued the day he ever heard it, he felt nothing now as he spoke the surname, nothing other than curiosity. He frowned. "What's Shari doing in Wisconsin? Last I heard she lived in Tucson."

18

"Oh, that was years ago, Bren." Karan's voice carried above the baby's squeals. "For the last, oh, I don't know, eight or ten years, Shari's lived in Florida."

"Awful about her husband," Miriam said, shaking her head and walking away. "Oh, and Ian," she said to Laura's husband, "would you mind shoveling the walk for our guest?"

"Sure."

Ian stood, and Brenan watched his mother's retreating back before glancing at Karan. "What about Shari's husband?" It had taken years for Brenan to stop hating the guy. But he could hardly be about the Lord's work with something like hatred in his heart. Long ago, he made the decision to give all those wrongful, painful feelings over to Christ. "What happened?"

"Don't you read any of my e-mails?"

"Well, I. . ." Brenan decided he couldn't lie. "I usually skim them, Karan, because I'm so busy."

His sister rolled her hazel eyes in irritation. "Greg died last March. He'd been sick for a long time. Abby told me he'd been out of his mind for the last couple of years and was confined to a nursing home. He used to swear at the nurses and call Shari all sorts of horrible names. But it wasn't really Greg. It was the brain cancer talking."

At another time, Brenan might have felt like justice had been served, but now, all he felt was sorrow. What's more, being a medical doctor, he could well imagine the particulars. "Must have been tough on Shari and all the Kretlows."

Karan nodded as her husband sat down beside her. "In spite of the big scandal they caused when they ran off together, Greg and Shari turned out to be committed Christians. That part has always made Abby nuts."

"Why?"

Karan handed the baby to her daughter, Laura. "Abby felt like Shari and Greg succumbed to the brainwashing she grew up with. Now, she says she doesn't even believe God exists."

"What a shame." Brenan narrowed his gaze. "So how do you know all this?"

"She does my hair." Karan grinned. "I see Abby about every six weeks, and we catch up on all the news."

"Ah." Brenan chuckled, but on the inside a strange, unsettled feeling filled his gut. Shari Kretlow Flannering, once the love of his life, was on her way over.

And she was a widow.

Chapter 2

Shari found the Open Door Inn easily enough and pulled into the back lot as instructed. She noticed other vehicles parked neatly in a row, although they were covered with white fluffy snow. She wondered if Miriam had guests after all.

Trudging around to the side of the house on a freshly shoveled walk, Shari reached an ornate wooden door. She stomped the snow from her black suede shoes and rang the bell. Miriam answered in a matter of moments.

"Merry Christmas!" The older woman enveloped Shari in a hug. "My, my, how good to see you again!"

"Likewise. Thank you for allowing me to stay here tonight. I hope I'm not intruding."

"You're not at all. Come in."

Stepping into the large foyer, Shari noticed the gold wallpaper and polished, dark-tiled floor. Miriam took her coat, and Shari watched as her hostess hung it in the front closet. Then she turned back to Shari.

"Let me get a good look at you."

Miriam gazed into Shari's face. Their height was evenly matched, and Shari noticed Miriam appeared older but still looked very much the same as she remembered her, with her rust-colored hair, brown eyes, and freckled complexion.

"I'd recognize you anywhere, Mrs. Sheppard."

"Please, call me Miriam." She smiled. "And I was thinking much the same thing. You still have that spark of mischief in your eyes."

Shari laughed, and the two clasped hands.

"Gracious! Your fingers are like ice. Come on into the living room and sit by the fire."

Shari thought she'd like nothing better. But when she turned to follow Miriam into the other room, her gaze found none other than Brenan Sheppard standing in the doorway. Tall, with ebony, short-cropped hair, he now sported a neatly trimmed dark beard. He only vaguely resembled the unmotivated college sophomore she had dumped for smooth-talking, ambitious Greg Flannering. And, judging by the way Bren's beige cable-knit sweater fit snugly across his broad shoulders, it appeared he had filled out his once-lanky frame.

Nevertheless, Shari was unsure of what to make of the situation. Was this a setup? A Christmas prank—courtesy of Mom and Miriam?

She chuckled at her deduction then decided to make the best of it. She stuck out her right hand. "Hi, Bren. Good to see you again."

His brown eyes regarded her outstretched hand before meeting her gaze once more. "After twenty-three years, Shari, I don't want a handshake."

She felt her smile fade. Did he intend to finally tell her off? She deserved it if he did.

Brenan grinned. "I want a hug!"

Within seconds, she was enfolded into a smothering embrace. She laughed, relieved by the outcome. Then, inhaling, she got an intoxicating whiff of Brenan's spicy cologne.

"Merry Christmas!"

Brenan released her, and Shari took a step back. "Same to you," she said. "I didn't know you were back in the States—not that I keep track of your every move or anything." Shari laughed at her sudden nervousness and quickly explained. "My church supports your mission team, and I read your newsletters every so often."

Brenan arched one swarthy brow. "What church is that?"

"Golden Shores Community Church in Pensacola, Florida."

"Sure, I know the one." Brenan's features lit up like holiday lights, and it was obvious he was enthusiastic about his ministry.

Miriam's voice interrupted their conversation. "Shari, come in by the fire. I know you're freezing."

Brenan turned sideways and extended a hand, indicating she should enter the room ahead of him.

Shari complied and walked into the cozy living room. Floral-upholstered furniture was placed in a half-circle in front of a glowing fire that crackled in the fieldstone hearth. One glance told her she had definitely intruded upon a family gathering. However, before she could utter an apology, Brenan's sister Karan jumped up from the settee and strode toward her.

"Shari! Wow, it's great to see you!"

Another hug, and Shari felt the sting of tears gathering at the corners of her eyes. These people should hate her, and perhaps they had at one time. But now, they seemed to have prevailed over any negative emotions, greeting her with such warmth and sincerity, it touched her to the very heart of her being.

Karan released her. "You look terrific."

"Thanks." Shari suddenly wished she'd stayed on her diet and lost those pesky pounds rounding her hips. "You look great yourself."

She did, too. Karan was just as tall and slim as during their high school days.

Totally not fair.

For the next few minutes, Shari was caught in a flurry of introductions. She met Karan's husband, Dan Strang, their daughter Laura, and Laura's husband, Ian. Then, at last, Shari's gaze fell on a towheaded baby, creeping around the plush carpet.

"That's my first grandchild, Chrissy."

"She's adorable." Shari smiled. Glancing back at Karan, she shook her head. "You're about the best-looking grandma I've ever seen."

Karan beamed.

"Shari, please sit down," Miriam said, indicating an armchair near the fireplace.

She did as the older woman bade her then stretched her arms out closer to the screen, warming her hands. "Maybe it'll stop snowing soon, and I'll be able to drive the rest of the way to Forest Ridge. I'm so sorry to infringe on your Christmas."

"The more the merrier," said Karan, reclaiming her

seat beside her husband.

Brenan sat on the sofa to Shari's left and Miriam on the other side of him.

"I heard the snow's going to keep up through tomorrow," added Dan, a nice-looking man in spite of his thick midsection.

His announcement about the weather, however, plucked an anxious chord in Shari's heart. She had no intentions of spending Christmas with the Sheppards, especially since Brenan was in town. It felt too weird.

She stood. "Maybe I'd better try to make Forest Ridge tonight after all."

Brenan pushed to his feet. "That'd be dangerous. You can't drive even that short distance in this weather."

"Bren's right," Karan said. "There's a winter storm warning posted for all of Northern Wisconsin, and the weather lady on the news at five o'clock advised folks to get off the roads and stay home."

"That was over an hour ago," Shari countered. "Maybe the snow has let up some. I did see a salt truck out on the interstate."

"Shari, I know we just met," Dan said with a grin, "but I'm a bossy guy. Sit down and relax. You're not going anywhere tonight."

Her gaze slid to Brenan who shrugged. Shari caught

an amused glimmer in his cocoa-brown eyes.

She sat, and the room fell silent except for occasional squawks from Chrissy. "Well, thank you for letting me wait out the storm here." She hoped she hadn't appeared ungrateful for wanting to leave. "I'm just looking forward to seeing my family."

"Understandable," Miriam replied.

"Especially after losing your husband," Karan added, a note of sympathy in her voice. "Abby told me about it after she'd returned from Florida and the funeral. Please accept our condolences."

Shari smiled back. "Thank you. I did get your sympathy card but never got around to responding."

Karan waved her hand in a dismissive gesture.

Brenan sat forward, resting his forearms on his knees. He cleared his throat. "I'm also sorry to hear about your loss. I just found out tonight that Greg passed."

"He would have learned the news sooner, had he taken time to read my e-mails." Karan sent her younger brother a withering look.

Brenan grinned back at her before returning his gaze to Shari.

"Thanks," she said once more. "But Greg's in a better place now."

Brenan replied with a thoughtful nod. "Are you okay?"

"Oh, yes. I mean. . .it was such a long, drawn-out thing," Shari said, settling back into the armchair. "But let's change the subject, shall we? This is Christmas Eve, and I already feel terrible about spoiling your holiday."

"Shari, you are *not* spoiling our holiday." Brenan's voice carried an authoritative tone. "So get that idea out of your head."

She saluted, and Brenan cast a quick glance at the ceiling.

Everyone chuckled, and Shari was again reminded of how much she preferred laughter to tears.

Karan stood. "Shari, would you like to see pictures of your twenty-fifth high school reunion? I got to go because Carol Baskin didn't have a date, and she didn't want to attend alone."

"Some things never change." Shari laughed.

Karan chuckled, too, but feigned an indignant stance. "Did you hear that, Bren?"

He rubbed his thumb and forefinger up and down his bearded chin. "I hate to admit it, but I thought the same thing."

After another laugh, Shari leaned forward and extended her right hand, her palm toward Brenan. He returned the gesture in a modified "high-five" slap.

"You two are despicable," Karan joked as she

sashayed from the room. "I'll get the pictures."

❧❦❧

"No, she didn't!"

Brenan chuckled as he watched Shari's incredulous expression.

"Vi Taylor married Lyle Koffey? But he was such a dweeb."

"It's the old ugly duckling story," Karan said. "Only it's the male version."

"Hmm."

Brenan grinned as he watched the two women examine the photos of the past summer's high school reunion. He hadn't been there because of obligations in Brazil, and Shari didn't attend, she said, because she couldn't take the time off from her work as a dental hygienist.

Brenan let the updated information on Shari's life digest as he continued to enjoy her exclamations over every picture. She found something hilarious about each one. Karan was in stitches, and Brenan had to confess to finding Shari quite delightful.

In many ways, she had changed a lot over the years. Gone was that intense, serious, almost angry young lady. Now Shari's disposition seemed more lighthearted.

Physically, she'd put on some weight, yet that only seemed to soften her all the more. Her hair was just as golden blond as he remembered; however, instead of long, she now wore it chin length, tucking one side behind her ear. Loopy earrings hung from her lobes, and matching bracelets clinked on her wrists. Shari might turn a guy's head, but not like Elena did. Elena's South American beauty could fill a room and draw gasps of awe from anyone in her vicinity. Part of Brenan reveled in the fact that he'd won the prettier woman's heart. Yet, there was something about Shari he found quite appealing.

He sipped his glass of hot chocolate and wondered what her life had been like with Flannering. Had she been happy? It appeared so. She'd said she loved him.

"Hey, Shari, did you ever have kids?"

The room grew quiet, and all eyes looked at him.

He glanced around at the stunned faces. "Did I say something wrong?"

"No, it's just. . ." Karan seemed to grope for words. "Where in the world did that question come from? We were talking about Ted Meinhardt's car dealership."

Brenan grinned. "Sorry. I wasn't paying attention."

Karan rolled her eyes. "Typical brother. He skims my e-mails and ignores what I say."

Shari smiled and turned toward him. "In answer your question, Bren, no, I never had kids. Greg and I wanted children, but they never came." Shari shrugged. "*Que sera, sera.*"

"What does that mean?" Laura wanted to know as she pried carpet fuzz out of Chrissy's chubby fist.

"What will be, will be," Miriam piped in as she re-entered the room. "Dinner is just about ready." Then she began to sing the old Doris Day tune. "*Que sera, sera.* Whatever will be, will be. . ."

Brenan leaned to the side, reclining on a throw pillow while his mother cantered down her own memory lane. He regarded Shari, and when she looked his way, he caught her gaze. "See what you started?"

She just laughed.

Chapter 3

At his mother's request, Brenan brought the Christmas tree in from outside and set it into its metal stand in a corner of the living room. Karan, sitting on her haunches, arranged the colorful, handmade skirt around it. As tradition dictated in the Sheppard home, the tree was decorated on Christmas Eve, and everyone helped. But first, Mom served a dinner of broiled beef tenderloin, twice-baked potatoes sprinkled with paprika, and French-cut green beans.

"Oh, this is delicious."

At Shari's remark, Brenan glanced up from his meal to look across the dining room table at her.

"You're a marvelous cook. Did I always know that, or have you improved with age?"

Miriam chuckled and winked. "I've always been a marvelous cook."

Shari smiled.

Karan cleared her throat. "Shari, did you hear the big news? Brenan's engaged!"

Her blue eyes widened. "No, I didn't." Her gaze flew to Brenan. "Congratulations!"

"Thanks, but they're a bit premature." He looked from his sister to Shari. "I haven't proposed yet."

"But you will, and Elena will say yes." Confidence shone on his sister's face. "You said so yourself."

"I can't wait to meet her," Miriam said. "This summer. . .right, Bren?"

He nodded.

"See?" Karan waved a hand in the air. "The proposing part is a mere technicality."

Brenan grinned. He supposed that was true. His entire mission team expected him to ask Elena to marry him. They were a perfect match, after all. He was a doctor. She was a nurse. They were both unattached and committed Christians. Besides, Elena was crazy about him. What more could Brenan ask for in a woman?

Still, he was sort of waiting for that love-struck feeling to hit him. However, he wasn't fifteen anymore and head-over-heels in love with Shari Kretlow, the pastor's kid. The more he recollected, the more he realized Shari had been one wild young lady back in those days. But Brenan knew why. Pastor Kretlow ran his home like a detention center. The more curfews and groundings he had imposed, the more Shari and her siblings rebelled. Shari had confided in Brenan about everything.

Hindsight told him that, although he had loved Shari more than his own being, she'd viewed him simply as a good friend. When he asked her to marry him, she accepted solely because she couldn't wait to get out of her parents' home. Brenan realized it now. He knew, too, that Pastor Kretlow had mellowed over the years. The man had always loved his congregation, but back then, he was a tyrant of a father. Even when Shari was in college.

"Brenan, I've got to tell you something."

Her voice drew him from his reverie.

"For years, I've felt burdened for you, and I've been praying that God would bring the perfect woman into your life. You know—it's not good for man to be alone and all that." Shari laughed, and Brenan grinned, catching her paraphrase of Genesis 2:18. Then, she dabbed the corners of her mouth with her white linen napkin. "I'm not making this up either." She shot an earnest look at Karan before glancing back at Brenan. "I'd be happy to show you my prayer journal as proof."

"I believe you, and it seems God answered your prayers." He smiled but felt oddly disconcerted. Wasn't Elena the perfect woman for him? When he left Brazil, he'd thought so. Why did he suddenly feel so skeptical?

"I'll also have you know this blizzard is my fault."

"How's that, Shari?" Miriam asked.

Brenan forked some potato into his mouth as he listened

"I like Florida, but I miss the seasons, especially snow at Christmastime. So I asked God for a white Christmas." She grinned. "God always answers my prayers, even though His answer is sometimes no. In this case, He said, 'Let it snow!' "

"Hey, that rhymes." Sitting at the end of the table, beside the highchair, Laura stopped spooning baby food into Chrissy's mouth long enough to laugh.

"Stop me if I'm being too personal," Brenan began, "but it appears you're a much stronger Christian now than when I last saw you. How'd it all happen?"

"Oh, that's not personal, at least not to me. As you well know, Dad preached the gospel all the time. It wasn't just reserved for Sunday mornings. I guess I sort of tuned him out. I got sick of hearing the same thing over and over and over. What's more, my impression of a Holy God was a Wizard-of-Oz-like figure. You know, the guy with the booming voice and big white face?"

Brenan smirked and cut off a piece of his meat.

"One night when Greg was away—" She paused. "He traveled a lot. Anyway, I started watching a Christian broadcast, mostly because I couldn't find another program worth viewing. I began to get curious and wondered what made the evangelist on TV different from my pulpit-thumping father. I watched the entire program and had tears running down my face by the time it ended. I realized the problem wasn't with my dad at all. It was with me."

When she paused, Brenan looked up and met her remorseful stare.

"I wasn't a Christian when you knew me—" Shari glanced around the table. ". . .when you all knew me. Oh, I could talk the talk, but the truth of God's Word never penetrated my heart until that night."

Miriam smiled. "Your mother told me years ago. I understand Greg accepted Christ, too, although it was sometime later."

Shari nodded.

Karan grinned. "Abby told me, although she says there is no God."

"I know." Shari nodded her blond head. "The

Christmas story has been lost on her—as well as the reason God came to earth and was born of a virgin. Please keep praying for Abby. For my brothers, too."

"Will do," Karan promised.

"Hey, wait a sec," Brenan interjected. "How come I don't know about all this. . .about Shari and her family?" He glanced first at Karan, then at his mother. "Why didn't anybody tell me?"

"I *did* tell you," Karan said in her own defense. "Tonight. Just before Shari arrived."

"You said she and Greg turned out to be committed Christians." He shrugged. "Guess that wasn't much of a surprise." He looked over at Shari. "I figured the two of you *were* Christians."

"Far from it, I'm afraid. But I wrote you a letter, Bren." Shari sipped her ice water. "Years ago."

"I got it." He stared at his plate and remembered how little comfort it brought him, how hurt he still felt after reading it. Still, he forgave her. Forgave them. "But I don't recall you mentioning a turning point in your life."

"Maybe you skimmed her letter like you do my e-mails," Karan quipped.

A soft chuckle emanated through Shari's pink lips. "I know I told you about it, Bren."

He didn't remember. All that came to mind was her apology for dumping him.

Chagrined, Brenan cleared his throat. "I'm not one hundred percent sure, but I don't think you wrote about your conversion."

"Maybe not. Those blank cards will only hold so much information." She looked over at him, and Brenan felt caught in her penetrating gaze. Remorse pooled in her blue eyes. "Sorry."

"No big deal." He sent her a good-natured wink, but like a hot spot after a raging forest fire, the love he once felt for Shari began smoldering somewhere deep within his heart. It was time to snuff out the last of those feelings for good.

After dinner, Brenan sat on the back hall stairs with a string of Christmas lights in his lap. He thought about phoning Elena in Brazil. Maybe hearing her voice would offset the sound of Shari's laughter. He glanced at his watch. No, it was nearing midnight. Elena sacked out early and rose at the crack of dawn. Brenan didn't want to disturb her just because he was having a case of nerves.

Extinguishing the remnants of his feelings for Shari

wasn't going to be easy. Already, Brenan felt he was losing the battle. Sitting across from her at the dinner table fanned some inexplicable eternal flame. After all, Brenan once said he would love her until the end of time. Back then he'd meant every word.

Lord, this can't be happening. . . .

He plugged the lights into a nearby electric outlet. Then, slowly, he began unscrewing each large colored bulb, replacing it with a new one in hopes of finding the culprit responsible for disabling the entire string. For as long as Brenan could remember, fixing Christmas lights had been his job—mostly because he was the only one in the family gifted with enough patience.

From the adjacent kitchen, the sounds of clanging stainless steel cookware, accompanied by the scraping of plates, reached Brenan's ears. He heard his mother's voice, then Karan's, and finally Shari's laugh. Odd, how the latter had somehow infiltrated his being and wound itself around his heart.

Lord, how can I still be in love with Shari after all these years? But, maybe what I'm feeling isn't really love. It's nostalgia. Brenan's resolve gained strength. *Right. That's it. Nostalgia.*

Brenan pondered the question and decided his emotions had run amuck due to the shock of seeing Shari again. And then there was all the reminiscing over those high school reunion snapshots. . . .

Chitchat began, and voices were raised over the din of rushing water from the faucet in the kitchen sink. More clanging and scraping. Brenan tried to ignore the ruckus and focus on the Christmas lights. Maybe he would make his excuses and retire for the night while everyone else decorated the tree. He'd spent a good part of the past twenty-four hours traveling. Spending the night in an airplane seat had left him exhausted.

And that's probably why I'm out of sorts. I'm overtired and not thinking straight. He grinned, congratulating himself on finally making the appropriate diagnosis.

"Oh, Shari, I never knew that! Honey, I'm so sorry!"

His mother's voice extricated Brenan from his thoughts.

Don't eavesdrop.

"Why did you stay with him?" Karan's louder-than-average voice rang through kitchen and into the back hall where Brenan sat. "I mean, if Dan cheated on me, he'd be dead, and I'd be in jail."

Brenan frowned. *Had Flannering been unfaithful?*

"Oh, honestly, Karan," Miriam said. "You say the most outrageous things."

40

"I'm serious, Mom."

"Listen, I had my own murderous thoughts. Trust me." Shari's voice wafted to his ears, and Brenan couldn't refrain from listening.

Someone shut off the faucet, and things grew quiet, including Shari's tone. Brenan suddenly had to strain to hear her.

"But I realized that I made a vow before God, for better or for worse, in sickness and in health, till death do we part, and I had to live up to that promise. Because I did, Greg became a Christian."

"Abby never said a word."

Brenan rolled his eyes at Karan's remark and unscrewed another bulb. He replaced it. Nothing. He moved on to the next light.

"I kept Greg's infidelity from my family, although they know about it now. But back then, I was afraid they wouldn't support me in my decision to stay with Greg. And I didn't want to stay with him, but when he returned home after his fling and said he'd been diagnosed with a brain tumor, it seemed almost inhumane to turn him away—especially since I carried the health insurance."

"Oh, mercy!" Mom exclaimed. "You've really been through the wringer, haven't you?"

"I refer to it as tried by fire." Shari laughed. "I like to think of myself as pure gold now."

Brenan caught her reference to Job's trials and tribulations in the Old Testament, and he couldn't help but smirk.

"Do you think you'll ever remarry?" Karan asked.

Brenan hated the way his ears perked up at that question.

"I don't know. It takes a long time to train a husband."

All three ladies chuckled.

Brenan rolled his eyes.

"Besides," Shari added, "the world is full of such weirdoes, even within the Christian community. That may sound harsh, but God warned his children about wolves in sheep's clothing. I'm here to tell you they really exist. Take the last date I had. Now, mind you I haven't dated in more than two decades, but. . ."

Shari's voice became nothing more than a whisper. Seconds later, shrieks of disbelief, followed by raucous laughter, bounced off the plaster walls and ping-ponged into the back hall. Brenan didn't think he could stand hearing much more. His emotions were in a jumble. His heart went out to Shari for enduring her husband's unfaithfulness without the support of her family. At the same time, he admired her strength of character. He suddenly wanted to know more about her. In a word, he was. . .interested.

All at once, Brenan felt like a guy who'd stepped into quicksand, and he was sinking fast. Up to his knees. To his chest. Soon, he'd be a goner.

Oh, Lord, help!

The string of lights in his lap suddenly went on. *Thank You, Jesus!* Yanking the cord out of the socket, he stood and traipsed through the breakfast nook. He paused when he reached the main part of the kitchen.

The women sobered when they saw him. Surprised expressions lit their faces.

"I think it's sin to have so much fun doing the dishes," he teased, careful not to meet Shari's gaze. He held the lights up to his mother. "All fixed."

"Wonderful. Thank you, Bren."

After a nod, he proceeded into the living room, hoping to busy himself. No doubt, Dan and Ian would help rid his mind of those unexpected, unwelcome thoughts about Shari.

Chapter 4

Shari wanted to disappear. "Do you think he heard us?"

"Naw." Karan sent her a dismissive wave. "Bren doesn't listen to small talk. I mean, think of how he tuned us out when we were looking at those pictures. We were all in the same room, and he couldn't even keep up with the conversation."

Shari hoped Karan was right, although she'd glimpsed an odd expression on Bren's face before he strode out of the kitchen. Had it been pity? Or was it satisfaction? Did Bren think it had all turned out for the best? He would have never gone to medical school if he married her.

"Elena, being a nurse, must talk his language, because. . ." Karan shook her head. "If women are from

Venus and men are from Mars, then Bren's got his very own planet."

"Oh, nonsense," Miriam said while loading the dishwasher. "Bren just has an incredible mind. Smart as a whip. That's why he's such a marvelous doctor."

Shari smiled, recalling he'd always been a good student. She probably wouldn't have graduated from high school if Brenan hadn't helped her.

Pushing up her sleeves, she rinsed plates and salad bowls while Miriam loaded the dishwasher. Then Shari washed the remaining pots and pans, and Karan dried them and put them away.

At long last, the ladies ambled into the living room. The first thing Shari noticed was Chrissy fussing in Laura's arms. Exasperation pinched the younger woman's features, and Shari's heart went out to her.

"Can I hold the baby?"

"If you want." Laura glanced at her daughter, then back at Shari. "She's awfully crabby. Happens every night before bedtime."

Shari gathered Chrissy in her arms, and Laura handed her a crocheted, pink baby blanket and a pacifier. The child squawked, but Shari rocked her side-to-side and began singing soft strains of "Away in a Manger." Chrissy quieted and stared into Shari's face. Seating herself on the couch near the fire, Shari wrapped the blanket snugly around the little one. She rocked and sang to the baby while watching Miriam, Karan, and Laura unpack boxes of decorations. Since she'd barged in on their Christmas Eve, tending to the baby was the least Shari felt she should do. Besides, she never passed up an opportunity to hold an infant.

Shari went through her repertoire of lulling Christmas songs. "Silent Night," "It Came Upon a Midnight Clear," "O Come, O Come Emmanuel," and her favorite, "O Holy Night."

"I don't believe it," Laura said much later. She crossed the room and peered down into her now sleeping child's face. "She looks so sweet and innocent. Who'd believe she's such a terror by day?"

Grinning, Shari thought Laura favored her mother in appearance, right down to her trim figure and hazel eyes.

"You got her to sleep." She stared at Shari. "How'd you do that?"

Feeling pleased, Shari shrugged. "I do have a way with kids. The nursery workers at church adore me."

"I can see why. Will you come and live with me and do this every night?"

She laughed, hearing the teasing note in Laura's voice.

Then, Laura moved to take Chrissy, but Shari touched her forearm. "Can I hold her a while longer?"

"Sure. Just holler when your arms feel like they're about to give way. Chrissy's a pretty solid kid."

"I'll holler, but not too loudly."

Laura's eyes widened and peered at Chrissy. "Right."

She returned to assist her mother and grandmother in trimming the tree. It already looked lovely.

Shari sighed. A glowing fireplace, a sleeping baby in her arms—life didn't get much better than this.

⚜

Brenan leaned on the heavy oak doorframe, his arms folded across his chest, and watched Shari rock his great-niece to sleep. Since he stood just outside her line of vision, he could regard her unnoticed, and Brenan couldn't help but feel a little envious of Chrissy, snuggled in close, the lilt of Shari's soprano voice soothing her into a deep sleep. In fact, Brenan's eyelids grew heavy, and he seriously contemplated making his excuses and retiring to his bedroom. But another tradition in the Sheppard family was reading the Christmas story from the Gospel of St. Luke. Brenan's brother-in-law had been awarded the privilege tonight, much to Brenan's relief. He felt so tired he could barely see straight, let alone read from the Bible.

Brenan blinked, seeing his mom's orange tabby, Sunkissed, hop up on the couch. The animal nestled himself next to Shari, and Brenan realized she had that way about her, attracting both people and pets. Greg was daft to risk his marriage for what Shari had termed "a fling." And Shari—she was one remarkable woman to take him back, and all to God's glory. Brenan couldn't get over it. He kept thinking about it, much to his irritation.

Before he had a chance to consider his actions, he walked to the couch and scooped up Sunkissed, setting him on the carpeted floor. The cat meowed, but Brenan ignored the protests as he seated himself beside Shari.

"Hey, that wasn't nice, Uncle Bren. Sunkissed was dozing."

He glanced at his niece, who held gold garland in her hands. "Would it have been better if I sat on the thing?"

"The *thing?*" Laura gave him a look of admonishment. "Sunkissed isn't a *thing.*"

"My apologies for the offense, Laura," he said with a smirk, "but I've always believed that furniture is for people, and obscure corners—preferably outside—are for cats."

Laura rolled her eyes, Miriam chuckled, and Karan

grinned before muttering, "Typical Bren."

Beside him, Shari grinned. "You never did like cats, did you?"

Turning to his right, he met her blue-eyed stare. "Nope. Never did."

Her smile widened at his admission before she glanced down at the sleeping baby in her arms.

Bren stretched his arm out along the top of the sofa and reached across Shari's lap with the other to caress Chrissy's soft cheek. "Babies look so angelic when they're sleeping."

"Yes, they do."

"And this girl is a very healthy little angel." He grinned and straightened. "But each time I look at her, I feel this inexplicable burden for an orphanage in Cambodia." Brenan didn't know why he was telling Shari all this, but it seemed the thing to do. "I heard about the place from a fellow missionary. Children, some as young as newborn babies, are left at the doorstep. Many are sick and need medical attention, but the ailments are usually curable."

Shari looked aghast. "They're left at the doorstep of the orphanage? Abandoned?"

Brenan nodded. "Usually it's a family member—a grandmother or distant relative—who has been left with the responsibility of caring for the child for one reason or another. Due to the extreme poverty in that country, many can't afford to pay for healthcare. Even if they could, qualified physicians are hard to find."

Shari's gaze turned misty. "That breaks my heart."

"Mine, too."

"You and Elena *have* to go."

Brenan chuckled at Shari's determination. "Well, we'll see." The truth was, Elena didn't want to leave Brazil and her people. Many of them were in as much need as the poorest of Cambodians.

"What's to see, Bren? Those children need you. God didn't put that burden on your heart for nothing."

He couldn't quell the smirk tugging at his mouth. Shari had always been something of an advocate for the underprivileged. In high school she befriended the kids others picked on.

Like himself. Brenan had always been the guy who wasn't good at sports, a little awkward and clumsy until he'd grown into his feet.

At that moment, Dan and Ian sauntered into the living room and sat down. Dan set his large, black Bible on the coffee table, an indication he was ready to read the Christmas story whenever Miriam spoke the word.

Brenan sat back and relaxed as light chitchat ensued.

Meanwhile, his mother, Karan, and Laura finished decorating the tree. A good while later, Laura took Chrissy upstairs to the portable crib.

"Remind me. Do you and Karan have other children?" Shari asked Dan as she smoothed out her black dress over her knees.

"Two sons. Both in the army." Dan's expression was a mix of pride and remorse.

"Broke their mother's heart," Karan said from across the room. "I cried for a week after they went off to boot camp. That's where they are now. But they should be here with us."

"Now, Karan. . ." Dan shot his wife an understanding glance. "They'll be back."

"How old are they?" Shari wanted to know.

"Eighteen and twenty." Dan shifted his weight in the armchair.

Moments of silence passed before Shari turned to Brenan. "Hey, Bren, tell me about Brazil. As I said before, I've read your quarterly newsletters, but tell me the inside scoop."

He grinned. "What inside scoop?"

"Well, what's your apartment or house like? What are the people like?" She arched a conspiratorial brow. "How'd you meet Elena?"

Everyone hooted.

"That's what she really wants to know, Bren." Dan laughed again.

Shari's face turned the color of her red sweater. "Okay, so I'm nosy. Everybody already knows that about me."

Brenan's smile grew, and Dan and Ian chuckled. "Elena is a nurse at the hospital where I work."

"And?" Shari prompted.

"And. . .what?"

"How did you meet? Was Elena walking down the hallway, taking care of somebody, what?"

"Actually, she was angry with an uncooperative patient and hurled an empty bedpan across the room. I happened to be entering at that precise moment to see what all the yelling was about. Fortunately, I ducked before getting clunked upside the head."

Shari burst out laughing, causing Brenan to chuckle.

Standing near the tree, Karan whirled around and strode toward him. "How come you never told Mom and me that story?"

"I don't know." He laughed again, mostly because Shari was still cackling next to him.

"Guess you just have to ask the right questions," Ian said with a toss of his blond head and a wry grin.

"So she got your attention, eh?" Shari's shoulders shook with amusement.

"I suppose you could say I got her attention. Elena felt so ashamed for losing her temper that she apologized about five times. Finally, she asked if she could make me dinner in recompense for her deplorable behavior. I agreed. Things progressed from there."

"Smart woman," Shari said. "She knows the way to a man's heart is through his stomach."

While others found the remark amusing, Brenan didn't. He studied the hem on his trousers. The truth was, Elena hadn't found her way to his heart. He thought she had, but it seemed someone else still occupied that special place.

He looked at Shari. Her blue eyes sparkled back at him.

"Did she do the whole soft music and candlelight thing?"

Feeling oddly mesmerized, Brenan found it hard to even muster a smile. "Candlelight? Yeah."

"You should have sensed trouble right there, buddy," Dan quipped.

Positioned directly behind him, Karan smacked the top of her husband's head. "Marriage is blissful, remember?"

"Oh, yeah. Glad you reminded me."

More chuckles filled the room.

"All right, everyone, I think it's time for the Christmas story." Miriam reentered the living room, and her announcement put a cap on further merriment. "Just as soon as Laura returns from putting the baby to bed, we'll begin."

Dan slid his Bible onto his lap and flipped it open.

Shari leaned closer to Brenan. "I'm sorry if I embarrassed you. Sometimes I get carried away."

"No harm done." He gave her a smile and moved his hand from the back of the couch to her shoulder. He gave it a squeeze—an effort to assure her. But seconds later, he brought his arm back to his side. He shouldn't touch her. He shouldn't even sit next to her. Even the same room was too close a proximity, and yet he couldn't get himself to budge.

"I'm really happy for you, Bren."

Her words crimped his heart, and he realized that somewhere in the deepest recesses of his being he didn't want Shari to feel happy about his impending engagement to Elena.

He wanted Shari to love him.

Chapter 5

A nd so it was, that, while they were there, the days were accomplished that she should be delivered. And she brought forth her first-born son, and wrapped him in swaddling clothes, and laid him in a manger; because there was no room for them in the inn.' "

As Shari listened to Dan Strang read from Luke, chapter two, she tamped down anguished thoughts of those poor children being left on the orphanage's doorstep in Cambodia. She tried to pay attention to the Christmas story but found herself asking Jesus to protect those helpless kids on the other side of the world. Wouldn't Shari love to tell *them* the Christmas story and about how much Jesus loves them! She would probably want to adopt every single child she met.

Maybe I could adopt one of those orphans. Would it be allowed, since I'd be a single mother?

Shari decided to ask Brenan about it later. Perhaps he could put her in touch with that missionary friend he'd mentioned.

She forced herself to relax and pay attention to the Bible reading.

" 'And, lo, the angel of the Lord came upon them, and the glory of the Lord shone round about them; and they were sore afraid. And the angel said unto them, Fear not: for, behold, I bring you good tidings of great joy, which shall be to all people. For unto you is born this day in the city of David a Saviour, which is Christ the Lord.' "

Shari marveled as she always did whenever the reality hit her. The Word was indeed God and became flesh in order to save mankind from sin and eternal death.

What a wonderful Savior to leave His heavenly home and become a human by the lowliest of births.

Shari felt her eyes grow misty as Dan finished reading. She glanced at Brenan, only to find his brown eyes regarding her with interest. Giving him a tentative smile, she wondered why he was staring at her.

She looked back at the others, thinking Brenan was still very much that quiet, introspective man she'd known so long ago. It gave her an odd sense of gratification to know that, in spite of the years of distance separating them, she could still draw him out of his shell.

When the reading was finished, Brenan touched her shoulder. Again, Shari turned to face him.

"Are you still a coffee drinker?"

She nodded.

"If I make a pot of decaf, will you have a cup or two?"

"I'd love it."

She smiled, and Brenan stood. She watched him leave the living room then wondered if now wouldn't be a perfect time to ask him about the orphans and his missionary friend.

Following him into the kitchen, Shari paused at the doorway while Brenan scooped coffee grounds into the filter. She took a moment to collect her thoughts, until Brenan saw her and grinned.

"Can I get you anything?"

"Um, no, but I wanted to ask you about that orphanage."

"Oh? What about it?" Brenan walked to the sink and filled the carafe with purified water.

"I wondered if I could get more information about it, specifically about the possibility of adopting a child.

I've wanted kids for so long, and it just never worked out before. But I'd be a single mother. Do you think this orphanage would consider me qualified and. . .first things first, does Cambodia even allow adoptions?"

"I think they do." Brenan poured the water into the automatic coffeemaker then flipped the ON switch. "Tom and his wife have already adopted two kids."

Shari tried not to feel too optimistic. How many times in the past years had her hopes been dashed when it came to having a child of her own?

Too many to count.

Brenan's smile suddenly widened, and he strode toward her. Without warning, he leaned forward and pressed his lips to hers. Shari felt his soft beard brush lightly against her face as the moment lingered. To her surprise, the kiss warmed her insides more than a cup of hot coffee.

"Merry Christmas," he whispered, straightening.

"Merry Christmas," she murmured back, feeling stunned by what just occurred.

As if in explanation, Brenan flicked his gaze above her head. "Mistletoe."

She looked up and gave a nervous little laugh. "Oh!"

He chuckled.

"Okay, you got me. I never saw it coming, and I

never noticed the mistletoe up there."

She glanced up again, and in that time, she felt Brenan's arms encircle her waist. Wide-eyed, she stared back at him. His dark brown eyes peered down at her, warm and rich with a hint of longing.

Shari put her hands on his chest, pushing him back. "No, Bren. We shouldn't."

He sobered then released her. "I know. You're right."

She saw a flash of hurt in his eyes and caught the sleeve of his sweater before he could turn away.

"Bren?" She frowned. What could he possibly be thinking by kissing her?

He swallowed before replying. "I guess it's seeing you again, Shari."

She felt heartsick at the idea she might have ruined more than just his Christmas Eve. "I'm sorry."

Brenan rubbed the backs of his fingers over her cheek. "And that's the problem—I'm not."

"But—"

Before she could ask him about his fiancée waiting for him back in Brazil, Karan burst into the room.

Brenan took a step back, and Shari suddenly felt like they were mischievous teenagers again, kissing on the sneak like they did at age fifteen.

"Mom made chocolate mint pie. It'll go great with

the coffee." Karan smiled at Shari. "Want to help me slice and serve?"

"Absolutely."

Shari cast a glance at Brenan, but he was already making his way back into the living room. She wasn't certain of all that had just happened between them, but one thing she knew for sure—Shari wasn't about to stand in the way of Brenan's happiness a second time.

❧

What in the world possessed me to kiss Shari?

Brenan sat on the sofa while conversation droned on around him. He didn't hear a word anyone said as he berated himself for being so impulsive. It wasn't his nature, and yet he couldn't seem to help himself. Shari standing in his mother's kitchen, under the mistletoe, her pink lips puckered in thought. . . She'd simply looked too good to resist.

Brenan glanced at the entryway as Karan strode into the living room carrying a large tray. He stood to help, but Ian beat him to it.

"Shari went up to her room," Karan announced while handing out coffee and cake. "She has a headache, and I can understand why. The poor dear drove all the way from Ohio today, and she's beat."

Brenan wasn't surprised at the news, but he would bet it was his kiss, and not a headache, that caused Shari to retire for the night. He'd be lucky if she ever spoke to him again.

"Ian, would you be a sweetheart and bring in Shari's luggage?" Karan placed a set of keys in her son-in-law's palm. "She needs the blue suitcase that's in the trunk."

"Will do." The younger man grinned and reached for his wife. "I never pass up a chance to play in the snow."

Laura smiled and took his hand. Together they walked off.

"Bring the luggage in first," Dan hollered after them. He shook his head. "Kids."

Brenan felt a tad envious of his niece and Ian just as he'd felt envious of Karan and Dan over the years. *Lord, it seems everyone has someone, except for me.*

"Do you think Elena would like the snow?"

His mother's question yanked Brenan from his self-pity. "I—I don't know."

"Hmm." Miriam furrowed her brows. "Something bothering you, Bren?"

"Yeah." He set his untouched slice of cake onto the tray. "But maybe I'll have a new perspective on things tomorrow. I'm exhausted." He stood. "I think I'll turn in for the night."

"We're not far behind you," Karan said, sipping her cup of decaf. "I feel pretty whipped myself."

Brenan forced a smile then kissed his mother and sister before wishing Dan a good night's sleep.

As he climbed the steps, he rued his foolish heart. Talk about perverse human nature! Beautiful Elena awaited him in Brazil. But, no, she wouldn't do. Instead, his heart longed for woman who didn't return his feelings—Shari, a woman who would never love him back.

Chapter 6

Shari lay in the darkened bedroom listening to the wind howl outside. She kept reliving Brenan's kiss. Odd, how his kisses hadn't affected her when they were teens. But tonight's surprise smooch left her reeling.

Even so, Shari was determined not to give in to her feelings. What's more, the realization that her premonition had been right all these years caused a swell of guilt in her chest. Brenan hadn't married because she'd hurt him so badly.

Oh, God, please heal his heart. Isn't he in love with Elena? If he is, then why did Bren say he wasn't sorry after he kissed me?

A gust of wind whistled around the Open Door Inn, and Shari snuggled deeper into the pile of quilts on her bed. Once more, she thought of Brenan, and it pained her to think her very presence wounded him all over again. As for herself, Brenan's kiss had awaked her senses. She couldn't recall the last time she'd been in a man's arms for a sweet, romantic interlude—and her last date with "Mr. Octopus" didn't count. What a sick twist of fate that now, when she felt attracted to Brenan, he wasn't available.

But, maybe he could be....

No! No! No!

Shari reined in her foolish thoughts. If she came between Brenan and Elena, the Sheppards would regard her as that same selfish, rebellious woman she'd been twenty-three years ago. Karan would tell Abby, and then Shari's Christian testimony would be at stake. How would she prove to her siblings that Jesus was as real as Greg's illness had been if Christ couldn't be seen in her life?

On that thought, Shari closed her eyes and allowed the exhaustion from driving all day to overtake her. Minutes later, she slept.

≈≈≈

The next morning, Brenan awoke early. He showered, dressed, and then phoned Elena. He hoped that hearing her voice would alleviate his doubts about them as a couple. But instead of Elena, her roommate Dori answered the phone. At twenty-two years old, Dori was the youngest on the team. Spunky and likeable, she taught school for all the missionaries' kids.

"Elena's not around. She left for the weekend with a group of the others. They're celebrating Christmas by skydiving over Rio de Janeiro and then hiking into the Amazon."

Brenan sat forward and frowned. "Elena's doing *what?*"

"Skydiving. Tomorrow they trek through the jungle." Dori giggled. "You know them, Dr. Sheppard. They're crazy."

Yes, he knew. That is, he was aware of the five daredevils on the team, but he hadn't thought Elena was one of them.

"You couldn't pay me enough to jump out of an airplane, unless it was about to crash or something."

Brenan grinned at Dori's remark. "Thank you for the information. Please tell Elena I called to wish her a Merry Christmas."

"Will do. But, um, is that all you want me to tell her?" Dori's voice suddenly took on a teasing, singsong tone.

He knew what she was fishing for; however, the only three little words Brenan could manage to say were, "Yeah, that's all."

He disconnected the call and sat back in the armchair in the corner of the bedroom. He thought about how well Elena and Dori got along and then struggled again with age difference between Elena and himself. And it wasn't her daring that troubled him. Skydiving actually sounded fun, and he'd already hiked through parts of the Amazon with a tour guide. It was Elena's apparent footloose spirit that caused Brenan to rethink his marriage proposal. He suddenly realized he didn't want to spend the rest of his life trying to tame an energetic and overzealous wife. What if he didn't succeed?

Lord, I sense that Elena is beautiful in more ways than just her physical appearance. She loves You. That should be enough for me, but it isn't. I'll admit my attraction, but I'm not sure I could live with the rest of her.

His heart suddenly reminded him that he was attracted to Shari Flannering, too.

I'm one hopeless mess.

<hr>

"You can't leave without breakfast!"

Shari blinked at her hostess's exclamation. Standing

in the kitchen near the back hall, her suitcase in tow, Shari had been all set to trudge out to her car, clean off the snow, and drive to her parents' house. She'd said good-bye to Karan, Dan, Laura, and Ian, thankful that Brenan wasn't around. But when she entered the kitchen to thank Miriam for allowing her to stay over-night, the older woman halted Shari in her tracks.

"I'm baking cranberry muffins. Karan made a delicious egg, cheese, and sausage bake. Please stay." Miriam wore a beseeching expression.

Shari's resolve crumbled. She didn't want to appear ungrateful, after all. "Well, it does smell awfully good in here."

Miriam beamed. "Let me get you a cup of coffee."

Minutes later, cup and saucer in hand, Shari was escorted back into the dining room where Laura was feeding baby Chrissy.

"I didn't think you'd get away that easily," Karan teased. "Mom has this thing about feeding people."

Shari laughed. "So I've discovered."

"And she won't let anyone help her cook, either, although she did grant me the privilege of creating my Italian egg bake."

"It sounds scrumptious."

"You'll love it, Shari," Dan piped in.

Karan relayed the recipe, and Shari listened with a smile while she sipped her coffee. The egg dish sounded easy enough to put together, and the fact that it could be prepared the night before only added to the beauty of it.

At last, Miriam brought out warm cranberry muffins. A short time later, she carried in the rectangular glass baking dish containing Karan's masterpiece. Then Brenan followed his mother into the dining room, and Shari felt a nervous little flutter fill her insides.

"Merry Christmas, everyone." Wearing black jeans and a forest-green cotton pullover, he glanced around the table until finally his gaze met hers. "Morning, Shari."

"Morning, Bren." Her face began to warm under his scrutiny.

"Merry Christmas, bro."

He grinned at Karan, and Shari almost sighed in relief when he removed the weight of his stare. But then, to her discomfort, Brenan took the chair beside her. As he sat, his shower-fresh, spicy scent wafted to her nostrils. She found it most appealing, and suddenly Shari felt doomed.

I'm going to eat to appease Miriam, and then I'm out of here!

"Let's all hold hands and ask the Lord's blessing," Miriam said from the head of the table.

No! Shari's mind screamed. But out of a sense of propriety, she smiled at Brenan and offered her hand.

He took it in a firm, but gentle, grip.

"Ian, will you pray for us?"

"Sure."

Please be quick about it. Shari bowed her head, closed her eyes, and tried to concentrate.

"Thank You, Lord, for this food and for family and friends. Thank You for coming to earth two thousand years ago and taking on the frailties of human form in order to save our souls. Thank You for. . ."

Shari wanted to groan as the younger man's prayer seemed to go on forever while her hand was held captive in Bren's.

Finally, Ian wrapped it up. "We ask Your blessing on this food and on this Christmas Day as we remember Your birth. Amen."

A chorus of amens rang out from around the table. Brenan gave Shari's hand a small squeeze before releasing it. His gesture seemed to zing up her arm and go straight to her heart.

Moments later, plates were passed as Miriam served everyone a healthy portion of the egg bake. Shari began to eat, forcing herself not to gobble so she could high-tail it out of the Open Door Inn and Brenan's disturbing presence.

"So, Shari. . ."

She glanced at the object of her tumultuous thoughts. "Yes?"

"What made you decide to become a dental hygienist?"

She swallowed the food before it stuck in her throat. "Um, well, I was working at a dentist's office as a receptionist and realized that with some additional training I could just about triple my wages. So I went back to school, got my license, and that's how it happened."

"Do you enjoy it?"

"It's okay." Shari sipped her coffee, hoping it would wash down her emotions. "Pays the bills."

"Bet you have a lot of them, what with Greg being so ill and all."

Shari looked across the table at Karan who'd made the remark. "Actually, I don't have a lot of medical bills. I'm blessed to have premium health insurance through my job, and Greg was awarded disability coverage through the State of Florida. Of course, I don't own a house. That was the first to go shortly after Greg got sick."

"That's right. Abby said you have a two-bedroom apartment." Karan wiped her mouth with a red paper napkin. "She told me it's in a nice complex with a pool and a clubhouse."

Shari nodded. "I'm very comfortable there, and somehow I squeeze my family into my place when they visit." She laughed, recalling last Christmas, when her two brothers slept in sleeping bags on the living room floor. Two nieces and Luke's wife crowded into Shari's queen-sized bed. Shari and Abby slept on the floor nearby so their aging parents could occupy the guest room. The next morning, however, none of the adults except Shari's mom and dad could move—although it was a great excuse for jumping into the hot tub.

"You've been through so much, Shari. I sense your trials have made you a strong woman." Miriam smiled while spreading butter on half of her muffin.

"Oh, I don't know how strong I am." She thought of how weak-kneed and nervous she felt at the moment, just sitting beside Brenan. She tried not to look for his reaction, but out of the corner of her eye, she saw him give her a smile.

Finally, Shari couldn't stand it any longer. She scooted her chair back. "I need to get going. Thank you for breakfast. Thanks for everything."

"You're welcome, dear." Miriam smiled. "So good to see you again."

"Likewise."

Brenan turned in his chair. "Before you go, Shari, why don't you follow me upstairs to Mom's computer? I'm sure she won't mind if I use it to print off information on the Cambodia ministry I told you about last night."

The adoption possibility. How could she possibly forget about those poor children on the other side of the world?

"Bren, of course you can use my computer." Miriam sipped her coffee. "Just watch that printer. It's been giving me fits lately. Jams up every so often."

"Thanks for the warning." Brenan slid his chair back and stood. Placing his palm beneath Shari's elbow, he helped her to her feet and guided her toward the steps. "Tom built a pretty elaborate Web site. I think you'll find it extremely informative."

"I'm sure I will."

Together, they climbed the steps and entered Miriam's large bedroom. In one corner was a nook in which a computer desk fit almost perfectly. Brenan booted up the machine then pulled over a second chair. Shari sat down, forgetting all about her anxious, fluttery feelings. Instead, she felt hopeful. God obviously had a reason for allowing her to stop here last night in the middle of a blizzard. Perhaps that reason had something to do with adopting a Cambodian orphan. Maybe the Lord would finally bless her with that one thing she'd never been able to have, no matter how hard she'd prayed. . .

A child.

Chapter 7

Engrossed, Shari explored the Web site. She learned Hollia's House, the Cambodian orphanage, was named after a little girl who had died of leukemia. Hollia's parents were part of the American mission team that began the work there a little more than five years ago. After seeing the smiling faces of some of the youngsters and then reading their stories of how they came to live at the Hollia's House, Shari wanted to adopt them all.

"Bren, you have to go. It says many of the children at the orphanage are in need of medical care—like Hollia who died of cancer."

"I know what the site says." He sat back and stretched his arm out along the top of Shari's chair. "Tom's been after me to join his ministry for the past three months."

Shari sat back, too. "Why the hesitation?"

"Well, for one, I want to be sure it's God's will for me. There are a lot of worthwhile causes in the world. I can't take on all of them."

"True." Shari glanced down at her dark brown corduroy slacks and began to fidget with a piece of lint.

"Reason number two, Elena doesn't want to leave Brazil."

Shari looked up. "Ah. Yes, well, I see where that might pose a problem."

"And that's not the only problem."

Shari watched Brenan stare at the computer monitor. His profile was so familiar to her, yet so strange, especially with the addition of that well-groomed, inky black beard. She imagined it would feel more soft than scratchy beneath her fingertips.

She gave herself a mental shake. What was she thinking?

Refocusing on their conversation, Shari's common sense told her to leave the subject of Elena alone, but she couldn't seem to do it.

"What problem are you referring to, Bren, if I'm not being too nosy?"

He turned and regarded her, then leaned closer, as if about to divulge a very personal secret. "For some time now, Elena has been talking marriage. Each time she broached the subject, I'd get what I can only describe as a check in my heart. I discussed the matter with my pastor who told me I've just been single too long. I'll get over it." Brenan took a deep breath. "I've been trying, but that check doesn't go away."

"Did you mention this to Elena?"

Brenan shook his head.

"That might be a good place to start."

"You're probably right."

"So what's the problem?"

Brenan expelled a weary sounding breath. "Talking won't fix one of my biggest concerns. It's the difference in our ages."

Shari felt an odd twinge of jealousy. "How young is she?"

"Just turned thirty."

"Thirty isn't that young, Bren." Shari quelled her envy. "But she's still got many childbearing years ahead of her."

She can give him a family, and I can't. Shari shook off her wayward thoughts. *Why am I even thinking about me? I have no part in this equation.*

"I'm not so concerned about the childbearing part of Elena's age," Brenan said, recapturing Shari's attention.

"What makes me wary is her rather irresponsible behavior. Elena acts more like she's twenty. I don't want to become some sort of father figure to my wife. If I marry, I want a partnership. Camaraderie. I think a husband and wife should be on the same emotional and spiritual plane."

"Well, yeah, that's the way it's supposed to work." Shari laughed and tore her gaze from Brenan's earnest eyes. "But I'm afraid I'm no expert in that area. For half my marriage, I was blissfully ignorant of reality, believing Greg loved me the way I loved him. But then, one day, I got this phone call—"

Shari halted.

"Go on," he urged. "Tell me."

Brenan's tone was filled with such compassion, that Shari didn't think twice about continuing. "One day I received a phone call from a woman named Annette Jenkins. She had just discovered Greg had a wife and, as a way of getting even, she decided to contact me and divulge the whole ugly truth about her fling with my husband. Actually, it was more than a fling."

Brenan winced.

"And here I thought he was away on business, working hard, missing me while he slept alone in his hotel room. The truth was he'd been staying with her. They even had an apartment together! Greg had lied to Annette, too, saying he was on business when he'd come home to me." Shari smacked her palm against her forehead. "Stupid me, I never suspected a thing."

"Aw, Shari, I'm so sorry."

"Thanks." She ran her thumbnail up and down the crease in her slacks. "But maybe I got my comeuppance, huh?"

After throwing out the challenge, she looked up and studied Brenan's face, gauging his reaction. All she saw in his expression was sympathy.

"I wouldn't wish that kind of heartache on my worst enemy." He slipped his arm around her shoulders and gave her a hug. In a soft voice, he added, "And I never thought of you as my enemy, Shari."

His gentle words, his nearness, and embrace seemed to penetrate her very soul. Lifting her hand, she touched his cheek, and then her fingers found their way to his silky beard. Their gazes locked, and Shari thought she could drown in his brown eyes.

But suddenly reality hit. *What am I doing?*

She shot up off her chair. "I have to go."

"Shari, wait."

She didn't, but instead hurried across the room and out the door. Running down the steps, she prayed

Brenan wouldn't follow. She found her coat in the closet, grabbed her purse, and called a good-bye as she hustled passed the dining room.

"Thanks for everything!"

"Whoa, Shari, wait up a sec."

She ignored Karan's request and grabbed the handle of her suitcase, still in the back hall.

"Good seeing you, Karan."

"But I want to ask you about New Year's Eve." She jogged through the kitchen to catch up. "Good grief, where's the fire?"

Shari's face flamed. "Don't ask!"

With that, she bolted out the door and to her car.

❧

From his mother's second-story bedroom window, Brenan folded his arms and watched Shari unbury her car. Snowflakes swirled in the winter air, and he prayed she'd safely make it to her folks' place before the next storm hit. As disappointed as he felt watching her go, a swell of hope plumed inside of him. He recognized the longing in her eyes. It had mirrored his own.

Shari's fighting the same battle I am. But why? Does she think all men are untrustworthy—like Flannering?

Brenan considered various scenarios and concluded

he could spend all day guessing. He'd have to pray. Only God could change Shari's heart—and his, too.

Lord, I think I still love her. Is that possible? Most of all, is it Your will?

"Bren, what did you do to Shari?"

Hearing the reprimand in his sister's voice, he pivoted toward the door and faced her. "I don't know what mean."

"Yes, you do. You scared her. What did you say?"

"Karan, I think. . ." Brenan stroked his beard and pursed his lips. ". . .I think we scared ourselves. Maybe we scared each other."

She narrowed her gaze and stepped toward him. "I don't get it."

He shrugged. "I don't either, but I'd like to pursue the matter." He headed for the door, skirting his sister.

"Pursue the matter? As in you and Shari?"

Brenan glanced over his shoulder and grinned. "Me and Shari. Kind of has a nice ring to it, don't you think?"

At Karan's wide-eyed, gaping expression, he chuckled all the way downstairs. Even as a kid, Brenan enjoyed riling his older sister. He especially liked to get in the last word.

Ah, yes, some things never changed.

"Merry Christmas!"

Shari threw her arms around her mom and dad, then her brothers and Abby and Abby's husband. Next, she hugged her sister-in-law, Rebecca, and nieces and nephews, Elizabeth, Crystal, Madeline, Andrew, and Johnny.

Shari expelled a sigh of relief. "I'm so glad to finally be here."

"Ditto. Your mother worried you'd get stuck in another snowstorm," Walt Kretlow said with a wide grin. At age sixty-nine, his hair had turned to silver, but Shari's father was still as tall and willowy as ever. The sound of his voice hadn't changed much either. It still rang with authority, although his features had softened. "Glad to see that wasn't the case."

"Me, too, but those last few miles were difficult. Roads are pretty slick."

Sylvia shooed everyone out of the delicious-smelling kitchen. Bread was rising in the automatic bread maker, and a roast cooked in the oven.

"When can we open presents?" four-year-old Madeline wanted to know. She had inherited Luke's blond hair and blue eyes.

"Soon," Sylvia promised her granddaughter. She

smiled at Shari. "The kids are so impatient."

"That's to be expected. It's Christmas." Shari hugged her slender mother again. "It's good to be home."

"It's good to have you home."

Arm-in-arm, they made their way through the small house and into the living room. Shari drank in the sight of her family, noticing two were missing.

"Where are Ashly and Simon?" she asked, referring to her brother Mark's kids.

"Deidre's got 'em," he groused.

Shari's heart did a nosedive, not so much because the kids weren't here, but at her brother's tone. Mark and Deidre were in the process of a nasty divorce and, judging from the last few times she'd talked to him, Mark was growing angry and bitter.

Lowering herself into one of the overstuffed armchairs with its red and green throw, Shari considered her younger brother as he sat on the couch. Remote in hand, he surfed the TV channels. He stopped when the kids squealed over a program they wanted to watch.

The phone rang, and Sylvia left the room to answer the call.

"So how was your drive, other than hitting snow north of Milwaukee?

Shari turned to her lovely sister-in-law Rebecca and

smiled. "Other than that, I made good time."

"How was your stay at the Sheppards' bed-and-breakfast?" Abby wanted to know. "Kinda boring, I imagine, with just Miriam there."

"Well, actually, Karan and Dan were there along with Laura and Ian and their sweet little girl Chrissy, and, um. . ." Shari turned and scratched the back of her head. "Brenan was there too."

"Get out of town!" Abby leaned forward, and under the lamplight, her hair had a purplish hue. Being a beautician, she was always doing something trendy to her short hair. "Brenan was there? Was it like World War III or something?"

"No, not at all. We got along great." *Maybe a little too great*, Shari added silently.

"You mean he didn't even make mention of how you dumped him?"

"Abby, that was a lifetime ago. Bren and I got along fine. Everything was fine." Shari hoped her no-big-deal tone belied the tumult raging inside her.

"Fine?" Mark pinned her with an incredulous stare. He sat forward and dangled his hands over his knees. "Shari, if I was Brenan I'd never want to see your face again, and if I did, there'd be trouble."

"Mark!" Shari blinked, shocked by his vehemence.

"I'm just being honest."

The minister in Walt Kretlow suddenly emerged. "Brenan is a Christian, Mark, and Christians forgive those who trespass against them."

"Yeah, whatever." He sat back on the sofa and crossed his legs. Shari thought her brother, wearing faded jeans and a gray sweatshirt, appeared rather disheveled. His light brown hair had outgrown its last cut, and his chin was bristly, as though he'd forgotten to shave this morning.

Mild trepidation gripped her. *He's letting himself go. He doesn't care anymore.*

"So, Shari, how is Bren these days? My, my, it's been a good number of years since I saw him last."

At her father's inquiry, she pushed out a smile. "Oh, he's doing just fine."

"There's that word again," Abby remarked. Sitting beside her husband, Bill, she arched a brow. "Somehow I don't think things were as *fine* last night as you say."

Shari waved a hand at her. "Oh, I'm tired, Abby, that's all."

Sylvia appeared at the doorway. She was all smiles. "Guess who just phoned? Brenan Sheppard. It was like old times, hearing his voice just like when he used to call for Shari."

She wanted to groan, but she kept a rein on her emotions.

Her mother looked right at her. "Bren wanted to make sure you arrived safely. He said he was worried about you. Isn't that sweet?"

Shari just grinned, willing her cheeks not to redden with embarrassment.

"He also said to tell you that he printed the information you wanted off the Internet, and he'll give it to you tomorrow at church." Sylvia clasped her hands with glee and peered across the room at her husband. "Isn't that marvelous? Bren and Miriam are coming to church tomorrow."

"Wonderful." Walt sported a pleased expression.

"I invited them here for lunch afterwards."

"You did?" Shari tried not to visibly grimace.

"Oh." Sylvia frowned, obviously sensing Shari's discomfort. "Shouldn't I have done that? I'm sorry. I thought by the way Bren talked that you were friends."

"We are." Shari groaned inwardly. "Listen, don't mind me. I'm exhausted and not thinking straight. Of course it's all right that Bren and Miriam come for lunch tomorrow. Miriam was the perfect hostess last night."

"Was Bren a good host?" Abby smirked.

Shari tossed her a withering look.

"Can we open presents now?" Andrew asked, leaning against his dad. The boy was Abby and Bill's eldest son, and Shari decided he was growing more handsome each year.

"Walt, what do you think?" Bill asked. "Can the kids rip and tear?"

Shari grinned as her father chuckled and nodded. "Have at it, kids." His gaze spanned the room, and he smiled. "Now that Shari's here safe 'n' sound, it's really Christmas!"

Chapter 8

The following morning, sunshine streamed into the room Shari shared with her niece Elizabeth. She figured it was just her bad luck that another snowstorm couldn't have been blowing through Door County right now, keeping Brenan and his mother at home.

Rising from the bed, she padded across the cold wooden floor and down the hall to the bathroom. She showered and dressed, changing clothes three times before deciding on a black skirt, white turtleneck, and a colorful coordinating button-down sweater. As she took care in applying her cosmetics, she tried to convince herself she wasn't out to impress Bren.

Yeah? Then why didn't I tell my family that he's got a woman waiting for him back in Brazil?

Shari stared at her reflection, hating the turmoil in her heart. She felt a stab of jealousy each time she thought of Elena. She had no idea what the lady looked like or who she was. However, Shari found herself secretly hoping things wouldn't work out for her and Bren. Then, she despised her wayward emotions all the more.

Oh, God. Shari closed her eyes. *I prayed for a wife for Bren, and now You've answered that prayer. Please let me be happy for Bren and Elena—and work in Bren's heart so that the doubts he told me about are alleviated once and for all.*

After a quick breakfast, Shari rode to church with her parents. Luke and Rebecca followed in their SUV, loaded with the three kids. Once they arrived, Shari helped her mother prepare two large urns of coffee for the brief fellowship to be held in the basement of the quaint country church following the service. Shari had forgotten how small the structure was. It seemed miniscule compared to the church she attended in Florida.

Sylvia wiped her hands on a nearby towel. "Well, that ought to do it. Shall we head upstairs?"

Shari nodded, but dread filled her being at the thought of coming face-to-face with Brenan.

"What's wrong, dear?"

Shari gave herself a mental kick before sending her mother a smile. "Nothing's wrong. Nothing at all."

"Sharon Rose, I know you too well." Sylvia's blond brows knitted together in a frown. "Something's bothering you. What is it?"

For about five seconds, she considered confiding in her mom, but then realized Sylvia would fret throughout the service and worry all afternoon. *No, best to keep things to yourself.*

Shari laughed. "I'm being silly, that's what it is. It's been eons since I've seen a lot of the people who'll be here today. I guess I'm feeling a bit nervous."

Immediate relief washed over Sylvia's features. "Oh, don't worry about anything. Folks wonder how you're doing all the time. Dad and I stay busy trying to keep 'em up-to-date."

Still smiling, Shari followed her mother up the narrow steps and into the tiny vestibule. Several individuals whom Shari didn't recognize were hanging up their winter wraps. While Sylvia stopped to chat, Shari wandered into the sanctuary. Already, her brother Mark had arrived and sat next to Luke, Rebecca, and their kids. Abby would show up soon with her husband, Bill, and their brood. While the minister's offspring rarely darkened this church's door, they had decided to gather together today out of respect for the Christmas holiday and their father.

Lord, You don't have to prove Yourself to anyone, but I ask that You would reveal Yourself to my sister and brothers. Please let them see that Christianity is real—that You are real!

On that thought, Shari traipsed across the quaint, country church. She chatted with several of her parents' friends, and then a gentleman whom Shari had never met started playing the organ so loudly it drowned out their discussion. Wishing folks a good day, she made her way to the front pew on the left side. It was the one her family had occupied ever since Shari was in grade school. Noticing that Abby had arrived and was busily seating her children, Shari looked for a place to squeeze in and still leave room for Mom.

At that moment, Shari glimpsed Brenan and Miriam strolling up the aisle. She hated the way her heart leapt at the sight of him, although he was a head-turner in his charcoal pattern suit coat, gray band-collar shirt, and black trousers. But she managed to smile a greeting.

Brenan nodded. "G'morning, Shari."

"Morning."

He grinned when she continued to stare at him, until Shari realized how stupid she must look and tore her gaze from his bearded face.

"Bren!" Abby's exclamation rivaled the organ. "My

long-lost big brother!"

He chuckled as she gave him a hug. Then, she pulled him forward and introduced Bill. Meanwhile, Mark and Luke stood and clasped hands with Brenan. Miriam was sucked into the throng minutes later.

Suddenly the organ quieted, but the welcome committee did not. Shari's father appeared at the pulpit and cleared his throat. Next, he grinned out over his congregation. "As you can see—and hear—my children are in attendance today."

Everyone chuckled, and Shari could tell her father was thrilled that everyone showed up. Tossing a smile at him, she turned to take her seat but realized there wasn't a space left for her beside Abby. *Of course, if Abby would kindly move her purse and scoot in closer to Bill. . .*

"No room here, sis. You'll have to sit back there." Abby indicated the pew behind her by thumbing over her shoulder.

Shari's gaze bounced to Miriam and Bren, then back to her younger sister's smug expression. "No problem, Abb." She wasn't about to let on that sitting beside Bren was the last thing she wanted to do. She wasn't about to appear rude either.

Stepping alongside the end of the pew in which Brenan sat, she forced a smile. "Mind if I sit here?"

"Course not, Shari." Bren slid over, forcing his mother to do the same.

Shari took her place. But the instant her arm brushed his, she felt doomed.

Abby twisted around and handed back Shari's Bible, still in its leather carrying case. Brenan politely reached for it and gave it to Shari.

"Thanks."

He smiled.

Shari's heart skipped a beat.

"It's also nice to have Miriam Sheppard here, along with her son Brenan. For those who don't know or may have forgotten, Bren's a doctor, and he's serving the Lord in Brazil as a medical missionary." Walt waved him to the platform. "Why don't you c'mon up and say a few words, Bren?"

Shari rose and stepped aside to let him out. Then, she claimed the spot next to Miriam so she wouldn't have to get up again.

"The Lord is really doing a great work in Brazil," Brenan began. "I've felt privileged to serve with the team over there. They primarily help the impoverished folks who live in *favelas*, or the slums. There's a real need in that part of the country." He paused. "But lately I've sensed God's call to a different part of the world, and I'd appreciate your prayers on this matter."

Shari saw him flick his glance in her direction, and something of a thrill spiraled up her spine.

"There is an orphanage in Cambodia that I'm burdened for. I'm acquainted with the man who runs it, and he's been pleading with me to come and help with his ministry. The children at the orphanage are in dire need of medical care. Here are some specifics."

Shari watched as he pulled something from the inner pocket of his suit coat. Was it the information he'd printed off the Internet for her?

"The orphanage cares for some one hundred and fifty children, but that number is growing by the day. An estimated one hundred and forty *thousand* children in Cambodia are orphans, having lost their parents to suicide, AIDS, and any number of illnesses and infections plaguing the malnourished and extremely poor in that region. Some children are disabled, like the twelve-year-old girl I was told about. She had been helping her mother harvest rice and stepped on a mine that was left over from the Khmer Rouge days. Consequently, she lost a leg. Other children live with hunger and severe malnutrition. They don't have homes, families, and education, nor do they have healthcare. They appear on the doorstep of the orphanage dirty and many times suffering with any number of tropical diseases."

Shari felt tears welling in her eyes. Her heart constricted as she listened to the plights of the orphans.

"A good number of the children come with behavioral problems due to the years they lived with abuse or neglect or both. In short, these children need Jesus Christ. They need to hear about salvation through Him. They need hope. Ministry goes well beyond helping to heal diseases and repair wounds. There is a spiritual aspect to it that I don't take lightly. But the question is, does God want me in Cambodia?" Brenan's gaze scanned the congregation. "That's why I ask you to pray—and please remember Hollia's House in your petitions also." He inclined his dark head ever so slightly in a show of thanks.

Shari sniffed and wiped the moisture from her tear-stained cheeks. Miriam handed her a Kleenex, extracting one from her purse for herself, too. Then Brenan sat down in the pew. He glanced over at Shari and sent her a rueful grin.

She dabbed her eyes. "You did a wonderful job up there—really conveyed the need of the hour."

He answered with a diminutive nod.

"I'm glad you and Elena are thinking about helping that orphanage."

Brenan leaned over and whispered, "Elena won't be coming."

"Oh?" Curious, Shari tipped her head. But, before she could inquire further, her father's voice filled the sanctuary.

"Thank you, Brenan. Now let's stand and sing our first hymn "Angels We Have Heard on High."

Shari stood, as did Brenan and Miriam and the rest of the congregation. From her vantage point, Shari caught sight of her brother Mark. His gaze lingered on her face before moving to Bren. Finally, he glanced at his hymnal and sang with everyone else, but Shari found the nonverbal exchange rather odd. What was Mark thinking?

It was then Shari recalled his struggle with forgiveness in lieu of the ugly divorce proceedings he faced. Perhaps he wondered how Bren could forgive her after she'd run off with Greg a lifetime ago. As she sang, Shari closed her eyes and prayed her brother and sister-in-law would reconcile. But first and foremost, she prayed they would become Christians. She also brought Abby and Bill, Luke and Rebecca, and her nieces and nephews before the Lord. Her desire was to see her entire family come to a saving knowledge of Jesus Christ.

But now, as the words of the familiar Christmas

carol tumbled from her lips, she couldn't stop thinking about the orphans in Cambodia. Her heart crimped with a longing to help them all.

". . .in excelsis De–e–o."

The song ended, and Shari lowered herself into the pew that suddenly seemed to have shrunk. Glancing to her right, she saw that Karan and Dan Strang, along with another family, now occupied the space on the other side of Miriam, forcing her to move over, which in turn caused Shari to sit even closer to Brenan.

To Shari's dismay it felt *way* too comfortable.

Chapter 9

After the service, Shari and Abby ducked out of church as the fellowship downstairs began. Brenan had been preoccupied by folks who wanted to hear more about the orphanage, and Shari had to admit she would like to have learned additional details. However, she had promised her sister they'd help their mom by preparing lunch before the Sheppards arrived. Now that Karan and Dan were coming to lunch as well, she and Abby would have to set two extra places at the dining room table.

"You know, I think Bren still has feelings for you."

Shari glanced at Abby, who placed silverware around the table. Following her with a stack of plates, Shari digested the remark and wondered how to reply. She had feelings for Brenan, too. But what about Elena?

She suddenly felt awful if she'd come between him and the woman God wanted him to marry. What would her family and Bren's family think of her now?

Except Bren did say he had a "check in his heart" about marrying her. . . .

"Shari?"

She looked up at Abby.

"You know what? If you and Bren got back together, I might even believe there's a God."

Shari was momentarily dumbfounded. "Why do you say that?"

Abby shrugged and set down the last of the silverware. "I always thought Brenan Sheppard was the perfect Christian—if there could be such a thing. I idolized him when I was a kid. He was like the big brother I adored when my real big brothers picked on me and teased me."

Shari smiled. "I never knew you thought of Bren that way."

"I did. And when you ran off with Greg, I hated you for a long time."

Shari winced.

"But I got over it," Abby continued. "I grew up. I learned Christians were more like our dad than Bren, and I learned that most romances ended like Romeo and Juliet's and not like the ones in fairy tales. Then I met Bill. He's a great guy, trustworthy, honesty, makes a decent living. I figured he was the best I'd find out there—and, don't get me wrong, I love him. But it's like I keep waiting for the day to come when he doesn't want to be married anymore, or, like Deidre, he decides he's got more important things to do in life than be a spouse and parent."

Shari wasn't sure what to say. She wanted to alleviate Abby's fears, but she didn't know Bill that well—and look what happened with Greg!

Abby walked around the table and came to stand right in front of her.

"I can tell that Bren's faith is real. I know Dad's is, too, even though he's made a lot of mistakes. But it's different with Bren. His faith shows on his face, and it's heard in his voice. I mean, when he was talking today about those kids in Cambodia, I felt like hopping a plane and adopting the whole orphanage."

Shari chuckled again. "Yeah, me, too."

Abby smiled. "And seeing you and Bren together today gave me some hope that maybe there is such a thing as everlasting love. I mean, he obviously still loves you. I saw it in his eyes when he looked at you. And you've been distracted ever since coming home yesterday saying everything was 'fine.' " Abby snorted. "Fine, yeah, right. I think you've got feelings for Bren, too."

"You're right. I do." Shari all but whispered the reply, fearing the fallout such an admission might bring.

But before she and Abby could discuss the matter further, the backdoor banged, and children's voices echoed through the otherwise quiet little house. The hungry troupe had arrived.

In the kitchen, Shari helped her mother ready the meal. She felt relieved that Brenan seemed to be giving her some space. He was hanging out with Mark and Luke in the living room and, judging from the chuckles emanating from that area of the house, they were enjoying themselves.

When at last they sat down for the noon meal, Mark was seated between her and Brenan. Once more, Shari was glad for the buffer. She felt herself relax and began to enjoy the company.

After they finished eating, there was talk of snowmobiling. Shari heard Brenan say that he'd brought along a change of clothes, suspecting "the Kretlow boys" would engage him in some sort of outdoor activity. Dan Strang opted to watch the football game on TV with Walt and Bill, and Shari decided she'd make herself useful in the kitchen again. But on her way in, she encountered her brother and niece.

"Daddy, you promised," Elizabeth said as large tears rolled down her cheeks.

"Oh, stop it. You go ice skating all the time."

Shari couldn't suppress a chuckle. "Luke, how can you not be persuaded by that sweet face pleading with you?"

He smirked. "Those are crocodile tears. She turns 'em on and off like the bathroom faucet."

"Dad-dy!" Elizabeth cried all the harder.

"Oh, you poor thing." Shari gathered her niece in her arms and hugged her close. "You're so mean, Luke," she teased her brother. "You broke your daughter's heart."

"She'll get over it." He narrowed his gaze at her. "Shari, for your information, all these kids know you're a big pushover."

"Well, of course." She stroked Elizabeth's blondish-brown hair. "What are aunties for? Now, what do you want, sweetheart?"

Shaking his blond head, Luke walked away, and Elizabeth sniffed. "I want to go ice-skating this afternoon. My friends'll be at the rink, and Daddy said he'd take me and Crystal."

"I'll take you."

"Goody!" The nine-year-old's tears vanished so

quickly, it amazed even Shari. Pushing out of her embrace, the girl ran through the house rounding up her sister and two cousins.

Luke appeared, dangling the keys to his truck. "Four kids won't fit in your car."

Even though there were five kids in the house, little Madeline was too young to partake of this outing, but Luke was right. Four children couldn't safely ride in her compact car.

Shari accepted the proffered keys, wondering if maybe she'd really been had by her niece this time.

Climbing the steps, Shari exchanged her black skirt and heels for black jeans and insulated hiking boots. When she returned downstairs, Bren was waiting for her.

"Want some company?"

The offer caught her off guard. "You don't want to snowmobile?"

He shrugged. "I thought maybe we could talk while the kids skate."

Shari's heart suddenly hammered inside her chest. Staring into Brenan's gingerbread-colored eyes didn't calm her in the least. She felt so torn, wanting to spend time with him, yet wondering if the idea was wise. Was a relationship between them God's will?

Everything was happening so fast.

But, then, gazing into her palm at Luke's keys, she figured it was foolish to forestall the inevitable. They had to talk. Their attraction to each other was obvious—so much so that even Abby noticed. Perhaps discussing things would help set them both in the right direction.

"Okay, come along." She smiled. "I'd love company and. . ." Feeling spry, she tossed the keys at him. "You can drive."

Brenan knew the way to the ice rink. He'd skated there himself as a kid, although now, according to Luke, a brand-new warming house had been erected, complete with a snack bar that served coffee and hot chocolate.

Driving through Forest Ridge, the town in which he'd grown up, Brenan noted the changes, some subtle, some not so subtle—like the movie theater. That building went up in the last decade or so, but the restaurant he and all his buddies used to hang out at in their high school days was still there, although its name was different.

"Do you have fond memories of this town, Shari?" he asked over the din of the chattering kids in the back of the SUV.

"Yes, for the most part." She smiled at him, and Brenan thought it lit up this cloudy afternoon like a ray of sunshine.

So how did he go about telling her what he wanted to say? He knew there was a chance Shari would reject him a second time, and he did his best to prepare himself for that worst-case scenario.

They arrived at the ice rink, and the kids ran for the warming house. In a flash, they had their skates on and were headed back outside.

Brenan purchased two cups of coffee and walked over to where Shari had found seats on the bleachers, which faced a large plate glass window in order for parents and spectators to observe and/or supervise the skaters. He handed her the steaming brew then sat beside her. He wondered, again, how he might begin to voice his innermost thoughts.

"Bren?"

"Hmm?" He glanced her way.

"You said this morning in church that Elena wouldn't be going to Cambodia with you—that is, if you even go. Can you tell me why?"

He almost breathed a sigh of relief. Leave it to Shari to get the ball rolling. "Sure, I can tell you. She phoned me last night from the hotel where she and some others on our team were staying. We wished each other a Merry Christmas, and then I told her in the nicest way I knew how that I wasn't returning to Brazil."

"What?"

He grinned at Shari's look of incredulity. "I'm not going back. Even if God closes the door on the ministry in Cambodia, I feel certain I'm not to return to Brazil."

"But what about your belongings? Don't you have to pack your stuff?"

"I don't have all that much, and what little I do own, the team will pack and ship it to me."

"Are you. . .well, are you afraid of seeing Elena again? Maybe seeing her again will stir up your feelings and—"

"No, that's not the case. I'm not afraid to see Elena." Brenan thought his "once-bitten, twice-shy" theory might be correct after all. Shari didn't want to get hurt again, and who could blame her. "I respect Elena, and she's a beautiful person—a fine sister in Christ. Last night I told her she's an outstanding nurse, and I feel privileged to have worked with her."

Shari grew quiet and stared out the window.

Brenan leaned closer to her. "But, Shari, I've sensed all along something wasn't right between Elena and me. Now I know what it is. I don't love her."

She faced him, her expression bordering on curiosity and trepidation.

He locked his gaze with hers. "I'm still in love with you."

Before Shari could reply, a man burst into the warming house. He glanced around, wearing a wild-eyed look, and began shouting. "Someone call 9-1-1. My daughter's hurt. I think she stopped breathing!"

Chapter 10

Here she comes. She's regaining consciousness."
Brenan knelt on one side of the child and Shari on the other. The little girl had taken a tumble on the ice, and someone behind her accidentally stepped on her fingers with their skates. Afterwards, she'd gotten to her feet but passed out, scaring the wits out of her father.

"Did she hit her head?" Brenan queried.

"I'm her mother—and no, she didn't," stated the woman who peered over them with a troubled look. "Angie was crying after she fell, but no sound was coming out of her mouth. Then her lips turned blue, and she collapsed."

"Could be that the pain from her injury caused your daughter to black out." Brenan gave the mother a little smile before looking back at the girl. He inspected her pupils before sitting back on his haunches. "Angie, can you hear me? I'm Dr. Sheppard."

She blinked and stared up at him with large brown eyes. At last, she nodded.

While Brenan continued his examination, Shari packed snow around the child's wounded hand. She guessed Angie's fingers were broken, although her thick mitten had provided a good amount of protection. The injury could have been worse.

A small crowd had gathered, and someone said the ambulance was on its way. Shari watched as Brenan interacted with the child. He assured her that everything would be okay. He asked what her favorite color was and if she had brothers and sisters. Answering his questions successfully distracted Angie, and she even smiled. When the paramedics arrived, Brenan and Shari moved out of the way.

"Thanks a lot, doc," the girl's father said, sticking out his right hand. A red ski hat with yellow trim covered his head, but his face was ruddy from the cold December wind. His expression, however, looked much calmer than minutes ago, when he'd entered the warming house.

Brenan shook the man's hand. "Glad I could help, although I really didn't do much."

Shari stood by, watching the exchange and thinking Brenan had done more than he realized. He had a soothing presence and an air of confidence about him, yet there wasn't an arrogant bone in his body. What's more, she noted that Brenan had a wonderful way with kids. It affirmed the idea in Shari's heart that he belonged in Cambodia.

Angie was taken off the rink and to the hospital. Normalcy returned, and the skating continued. Shari's nieces and nephews wanted to skate awhile longer, so she and Brenan headed for the warming house again. Several people inside approached them, asking what had happened, and Shari felt relieved she didn't have to reply to Brenan's earlier admission.

He's still in love with me.

Shari could hardly say she was surprised. She'd suspected it since Christmas Eve. But her mind was in a whir. She couldn't think straight.

When at last they returned to Shari's folks' house, they discovered Karan and Dan had left, and they'd taken Miriam with them.

"Looks like you're stuck here for dinner," Walt told Brenan with a chuckle.

He replied with a good-natured shrug. "If dinner is as tasty as lunch, I'm a happy man."

Shari watched her mother's cheeks turn pink from the compliment.

"Shari can drive you home later," Walt said.

"Well," Brenan hesitated and flicked a glance in her direction. "Only if she doesn't mind."

"Of course I don't mind, silly." She rapped him on the upper arm before sauntering off to the kitchen. But her easy reply belied the knot in the pit of her stomach. What on earth was the matter with her?

Dinnertime arrived, they ate, and afterward, Shari carried a tray of iced and decorated Christmas cookies into the dining room. She spotted Brenan outdoors on the patio talking with Mark, who smoked a cigarette. She noticed her brother appeared very attentive to whatever Bren was saying.

"Shari, did you just hear me?"

She shook herself. "What?"

Luke chuckled. "I said Bren's a great guy."

Her heart did a flip, but she managed to set down the dessert tray without knocking something over. "Yeah, he is."

Abby's words from earlier in the day came back to Shari. *Seeing you and Bren together today gave me some hope that maybe there is such a thing as everlasting love.*

Her family would approve of the match. Shari felt

certain of that now. She turned back to where Brenan and Mark still stood outside. Could it be God was answering her prayers with regard to family members . . .and He was using Bren?

Sometime later, Shari stuck her key in the ignition of her car and fired up the engine. She didn't even reach the highway before the words poured from the depth of her soul.

"Bren, I don't know what's happening."

"What do you mean?"

"I mean about us. You said you still love me, but—"

"Shari, I realize I put you in a bad position, and I'm sorry. But I can't help how I feel, and I thought you needed to know."

She mulled it over as she drove to the Sheppard's bed-and-breakfast. They rode for miles in silence.

At last they reached the Open Door Inn. Shari parked and, before she could say another thing, Brenan reached over and set his hand on top of hers.

"Thanks for the lift home. Maybe we'll talk sometime this week." He opened the car door and hopped out so fast, it jarred Shari's senses. She didn't want to part on such an uncertain note.

"Brenan, wait." She killed the motor and climbed from behind the wheel. She watched as he backtracked until he stood just a foot away, his hands stuffed into the pockets of his navy blue down jacket.

"You didn't put me in any sort of bad position. I'm just confused, I guess. You're a wonderful guy, and we have so much in common. We're both burdened for the same ministry, and we love children, but. . ." She wracked her brain, searching for the right words to express all the tumult inside of her. "Oh, Bren, I think I'm falling in love with you, but I'm just like. . .well, I. . ."

Brenan stepped closer, pulled his hands from his pockets, and cupped her face. His palms felt warm against her cold cheeks. "Shari, I would never hurt you. I'd die before I would ever break your heart. You don't ever have to worry about that from me, okay?"

She nodded as tears clouded her vision. She knew he spoke the truth. "But what about your mom and sister? Will they think I'm the same selfish woman who hurt you once and am now ruining your chances of happiness with Elena?"

"What?" Brenan brought his chin back, looking shocked. "My mother and Karan love you, Shari. They always have. I talked to my family last night after getting off the phone with Elena. Mom said she'd known all along that I still loved you."

His words were like a healing salve on her wounded spirit. "Bren, I think I love you, too."

Beneath the glow of the outdoor light Shari watched him grin. "I know. You said that already."

He kissed her and folded her into an embrace. Shari felt more cherished and secure than she could ever remember.

"I swear I'll never hurt you again, Bren."

"I'm not worried." He rested his temple against the side of her head. "And I'm not in any hurry either. I've waited this long for you, Shari. . .I can wait a little longer until you're sure you love me, and you don't just *think* you do."

She smiled, deciding Brenan Sheppard was a rare gem, a golden nugget along a stony pathway.

Suddenly, Shari felt moisture on her lashes and cheeks. She blinked and looked up. Fat snowflakes swirled in the frosty night air and landed on her nose and in her eyes.

"What is it with this stuff?" Shari stepped back and gazed into Brenan's bearded face. "It's snowing again!"

"Yeah, looks like you're stranded here."

Shari laughed. The light snowfall was hardly a major winter storm.

Brenan nodded, indicating the bed-and-breakfast behind them. "Plenty of room at this inn."

Realizing there was nowhere else she'd rather be than curled up beside Brenan while a fire blazed in the hearth, she hooked her arm through his. "You know, I think you're right. I'd better not drive in this *blizzard*."

"Right. Smart move."

Arm-in-arm, they walked to the house, and Shari thought of the tune she'd heard on the radio a few nights ago. She hummed a few bars and then, together, she and Brenan sang, "Let it snow, let it snow, let it snow!"

SYLVIA'S CHOCOLATE MINT CHRISTMAS PIE

Crust

1¼ c. all-purpose flour
½ t. salt
½ c. (1 stick) chilled butter, cut into small pieces
2–3 t. ice water

1. Mix together flour and salt. Cut butter into flour mixture until crumbly.
2. Add water, one tablespoon at a time, tossing with a fork until a soft dough forms. Shape dough into a flat disk, wrap in plastic, and chill for one hour.
3. After an hour, roll dough and fit into 9-inch pie pan. Trim edges, leaving 1-inch overhang. Make a fluted edge. Chill again, this time for thirty minutes.
4. Preheat oven to 375ºF. Bake crust for approximately twenty-five minutes, until very light golden brown. Cool slightly. Reduce oven temperature to 325°F for filling.

Filling

1½ c. sugar
½ c. (1 stick) butter

2 oz. (2 squares) semisweet chocolate, coarsely
    chopped
3 large eggs
1 t. white vinegar
1 t. peppermint extract
Dash of salt

1. Prepare filling by first mixing sugar and butter in
    medium saucepan, stirring until sugar has dis-
    solved. Remove from heat. Add chocolate. Stir
    until melted and mixture is smooth. Next add
    eggs, vinegar, peppermint, and salt. Stir well and
    pour filling evenly into prepared piecrust.
2. Bake for 35–40 minutes at 325°F. When done,
    allow pie to cool and serve it topped with a dollop
    of whipped cream.

Andrea Boeshaar has been married for over twenty-five years. She and her husband, Daniel, have three valiant adult sons and two precious daughters-in-law. Andrea has written articles, devotionals, and over a dozen novels for **Heartsong Presents** as well as numerous novellas for Barbour Publishing. She is the author of the highly acclaimed Faded Photographs series, which includes the following three women's fiction titles: *Broken Things, Hidden Things,* and *Precious Things.* For more about Andrea and for a listing of all her books, log onto her Web site at: www.andreaboeshaar.com.

CHRISTMAS IN THE CITY

by Debby Mayne

Dedication

I'd like to dedicate this story to Lori Welch,
a faithful follower of Christ,
who offers comfort and kindness to her friends.

Acknowledgments

Thanks to Rev. Fred Bouton for sharing
the details about prison ministries in New York.
Thanks to Rev. Scott Welch for offering
such great sermons and inspirational wisdom.

*Blessed be God, even the Father of our Lord Jesus Christ,
the Father of mercies, and the God of all comfort;
who comforteth us in all our tribulation, that we may
be able to comfort them which are in any trouble, by the
comfort wherewith we ourselves are comforted of God.*

2 CORINTHIANS 1:3–4

Chapter 1

No other student in the Northeast Culinary Institute could create a raspberry soufflé that came close to Kathryn Anderson's. In fact, her entire final exam—spinach crepes with crab dressing, chicken asparagus soup, fresh-baked multigrain bread, ginger shrimp, and raspberry soufflé—won top honors across the board. Kathryn was on her way to realizing her dream of becoming a world-class chef.

"Hey, Kathryn," Peter Townsley whispered from behind, "wanna go out with the rest of us tonight? We figured we might as well celebrate before anyone has to leave."

"Sorry, Peter, but I can't. I promised my aunt I'd come to her place after the exam."

Peter nodded his understanding and smiled. "Tell

Miss Celia I said hi. She makes the best homemade biscuits I've ever tasted."

"Will do." After Kathryn finished cleaning her section of the training kitchen, she joined the other students and waited for the verdict.

Three hours later, Kathryn walked past Rockefeller Center Plaza, her coveted certificate secured in the briefcase she clutched at her side. She'd won the dessert competition as well as best overall. Aunt Celia would be so proud.

Who would've imagined that Kathryn Anderson, daughter of Bette Anderson, queen of dinner theater in Boise, Idaho, would have so much as even thought of being a chef? Her mother was the least domestic person she knew, but summers spent at Aunt Celia's boardinghouse in Soho had given Kathryn a hint of what she wanted to do with her life.

Workers scurried around the plaza steps, getting the gargantuan Christmas tree ready for the lighting ceremony that would take place in a few nights. She inhaled deeply, taking in the scent of impending snow. Just maybe this would be a white Christmas—most likely Kathryn's last, since she'd agreed to an apprenticeship in the kitchen of the Don Cesar in St. Petersburg, Florida. Although she looked forward to the sun and sandy beaches, she'd miss the change of seasons.

The subway was crowded with holiday shoppers, most of them toting bags with store logos emblazoned on the sides. She hadn't even begun her shopping yet, but she would soon—before she left New York.

Once aboard the train, Kathryn found herself daydreaming about having her own kitchen, creating delectable delights for the most discriminating diners. As the subway train slid to a stop at the Houston station, Kathryn edged toward the door. She stepped off and took a quick glance around, enjoying all the sights and sounds of the city. This had been her home for three years, and she'd loved every minute of it.

Since Aunt Celia's place was only four blocks from the station, Kathryn walked the distance, looking right and left, nodding to shopkeepers who stood in their doorways, glancing up at the sky. Kathryn inhaled deeply and allowed the cold, crisp air to fill her lungs as she rounded the last corner, heading toward her aunt's. She was still amazed that Aunt Celia had continued to hold out on selling the last of the boardinghouses in trendy Soho, since real estate had shot sky-high. The three-story stone house with the wraparound porch immediately came into full view.

She blinked. Rev. Stan Jarrett, one of Aunt Celia's

regulars, stood on the front porch, wearing an expression of anticipation and looking more handsome than ever.

"Hello, Kathryn," the man said as she drew closer. "I've been watching for you."

"Why?" she asked. "Where's Aunt Celia?"

He nodded toward the front door. "Let's go inside. We need to talk."

A quick knot formed in her stomach.

Once inside, the entire downstairs of the house seemed eerily quiet, opposite of how it had been the last time she'd been there.

"Have a seat," he said as he rubbed his chin.

"What's going on, Rev. Jarrett?" she asked.

"Please call me Stan." The hint of smile quickly faded. "I have some disconcerting news."

"Bad news?" Kathryn's insides tightened.

He glanced over his shoulder, and Kathryn followed his line of vision to see Mona and Bonnie, two of Aunt Celia's valued and trusted workers, standing in the doorway, their eyes round, and their bodies tense with anticipation. Stan turned back to her.

"Your aunt had to be taken to the hospital this morning," he blurted.

"Hospital?" she shrieked. "What happened? What's wrong?"

"She broke her hip, twisted her ankle, and dislocated her arm," Stan replied.

Kathryn sank back in her seat. "How did that happen?"

"According to her, she slipped on the ice on the bottom step when she was taking out the garbage," Stan replied. "No one saw it happen. She said she lost her breath, but you wouldn't have known it, hearing her scream."

"She screamed?"

"Oh, yes," Mona replied as she stepped closer, filling the room with her expansive presence. "Miss Celia has a strong set of lungs. The fall didn't change that one bit."

Kathryn quickly stood. "I need to go see her."

"I'll go with you," Stan said. "But first, we need to discuss this place."

"This place?" Kathryn repeated, gesturing around the room. Then she realized that without her aunt here, there was no one to run the boardinghouse. Both Mona and Bonnie had families, so they went home after all the dishes were washed and put away.

"I realize it might put a crimp in your plans, but I was hoping you'd stick around for a while, at least until your aunt gets back on her feet."

Images of sun and sandy beaches flitted through Kathryn's mind as she wrestled with her decision. She knew what she wanted, but she also knew what would be the right thing to do. Aunt Celia had led her to the Lord at a very young age. No way would Kathryn let Aunt Celia down.

"Of course, I'll hang around here until she's better," Kathryn said emphatically.

Stan grinned. "That's what I thought you'd say. Ready to pay her a visit?"

Kathryn offered a stiff nod as she stood on shaky legs.

"Let me peek into the kitchen," she said. "We might need to pick up a few things on the way back from the hospital."

"Take your time," he told her. "Miss Celia's not going anywhere."

<hr />

Stan fully understood what Kathryn must be feeling at this moment. He'd experienced enough disappointment of his own. He could see the frustration on her face, and he felt protective of the diminutive strawberry blond. He'd forced himself not to act on his attraction to Miss Celia's niece in the past.

"We're running low on sugar and eggs," Kathryn said as she exited the kitchen. "I don't know why Aunt Celia doesn't have more delivered."

"She's been doing this a long time," Stan reminded

her. "I think she probably knows how to run this place with her eyes closed."

Kathryn now sported a frown but didn't say a word. He knew she needed time to mentally adjust to this change of plans.

They walked all the way to the hospital in the blustery winds that whipped around the cold, gray buildings. Awnings, which had protected shoppers in the hot summer, now flapped and made slapping sounds. Kathryn didn't seem to be aware of the world around her as she leaned into the wind and forged ahead.

Finally, she slowed her pace. "Which do you think would be better for dinner tomorrow night—marinated lamb served with a mint and basil sauce or shrimp served on a bed of fresh arugula?"

"What's wrong with fried chicken or pork chops?"

"You're kidding, right?"

"No, I'm not kidding. People come to Miss Celia's for home cooking, not gourmet fare. They can get the fancy stuff anywhere else."

"Well, I think they'd appreciate something a little different. We can stop off at a butcher on the way back."

Stan decided not to argue. "Fine with me. I'll eat anything you put in front of me."

She tossed him a look he couldn't interpret, so he

didn't worry about it. If she was mad, she'd get over it. If she wanted answers, she needed to ask the questions.

Miss Celia was propped up in bed when they walked into her room. "Hey, you two. I hear the weather's awful."

"You should know, Miss Celia," Stan said. "Gotta stay off those icy steps."

She grimaced. "Don't I know it." Then she turned to Kathryn. "I sure hope this isn't too much of an inconvenience for you to help out for a few weeks—at least until I can come home."

Stan quickly glanced at Kathryn to see her response. To his surprise, she didn't give away any of the frustration he'd seen earlier. She shook her head and genuinely smiled at her aunt. "No, of course not, silly. I'm more than happy to help out."

"Are you sure, Kathryn?" Miss Celia asked.

"You know I don't lie. Relax. Everything's under control."

A smile widened Miss Celia's face. "You're such a good girl." She glanced at Stan. "Take care of her, okay?"

He started to promise to do just that, but he noticed how Kathryn's entire body tensed. Kathryn spoke up.

"I'm perfectly capable of taking care of myself and your boardinghouse, Aunt Celia. Now get some rest so you can heal. Let me know if there's anything I can do."

Miss Celia chuckled. "Bossy little thing, isn't she?"

He didn't comment. He knew better.

On the way back to Miss Celia's City House, they found a butcher who stayed open late. Stan watched in amazement as Kathryn expertly placed her order and put it on a tab.

He waited until they left before he asked, "Wasn't that sort of expensive?"

"Maybe a little, but it's not like I'll have to do that every day. Starting tomorrow, I'll be doing all the ordering from the wholesale warehouse."

They arrived back at the house to find everything clean and put away. A note from Mona said there were two plates of leftovers in the refrigerator.

"You'll be working hard tomorrow," Stan said. "Sit down and let me serve you."

She paused then nodded. He was by her side five minutes later with two steaming plates of food and mugs of tea.

"How long will you be here this time, Stan?" Kathryn asked, between bites of food.

"I'm not sure. I'm still on loan from Nashville, but the prison ministry here needs people."

She suddenly started choking and coughing. "Prison ministry? What is that?"

Chapter 2

Y ou didn't know that's what I did?"

"I knew you were a pastor, but I've never heard of a prison ministry. What, exactly, do you do?"

He paused to consider whether to give her the long or the short version and decided on the latter. "I visit inmates in prison to let them know that they still have hope through Christ."

"Why would you do that?"

Her words gave away her lack of understanding, so he knew he needed to tread lightly on the subject. "Everyone needs to know about Christ."

She held her mug a few inches from her lips. "I know that's what the Bible says, but I can't imagine criminals actually paying attention to the Bible."

She obviously didn't know about his past.

Kathryn's eyes had begun to droop. He stood and nodded to the door.

"Why don't you go on to your room and get some rest while I clean up?" he told her. "We can talk after breakfast in the morning."

"Are you sure you don't mind?" she asked.

"Positive. I want to do it."

Without an argument, she nodded. "I am pretty sleepy. It's been a long day."

Stan wasn't sleepy, so he headed back to the hospital for a quick visit with Miss Celia. The wind had died down, and it didn't feel nearly as cold.

"I knew you'd be back," Miss Celia said with a twinkle in her eye when he walked into her room.

"You're a smart woman."

"Think you can work on my niece while you're around, Stan?"

"Work on her? What do you mean?"

Celia cleared her throat as she gathered her thoughts. When she spoke, the words were deliberate and strong.

"My niece is very sweet, but she's rather misguided. Unfortunately, my brother was a lousy father to her. She has trust issues because he was never completely honest with her. When she found out some of his long absences were spent in jail, she was very hurt."

Stan should have figured as much.

"Was he a guilty man?" he asked.

"Unlike you, yes."

"That's awful."

"I know. I'm also concerned about her walk with the Lord. She goes to church with me as often as she can, but I'm not sure how deep her faith is."

"I'll see what I can do."

"She believes in God, so it shouldn't be too hard."

"That's a good start, I agree," he said with a nod. "But what does she understand about the gospel message?"

"Not much, I'm afraid. Whenever I try to bring it up, she has to run off somewhere. I'm sure her reasons are legitimate. Still, it's hard to witness to someone who has one foot out the door."

"Yes, I know," he agreed. "It took a prison term for me to stay still long enough to listen."

Miss Celia looked him in the eye. "That should have never happened to such a nice young man as you."

"I agree. And that leads to another subject. What, exactly, does Kathryn know about my past? She seemed shocked when I said I had a prison ministry."

Miss Celia tightened her lips and folded her hands.

"Not much. Just that you're in the ministry, and you travel quite a bit."

"I guess I need to tell her about my prison term and a few of the details if I'm going to stay in the house with her in charge."

"It'll come as a shock to her."

"You're right. I'll be very careful how I tell her. Hopefully, I won't scare her too much. In the meantime, you need to concentrate on healing."

Her eyes quickly misted. "I feel awful that I won't be able to make it to her graduation ceremony."

He patted her hand. "I'm sure she understands, Miss Celia." He straightened and moved toward the door.

"Come back and see me soon, okay, Stan?"

"Yes, of course," he said as he left the room. As he stepped outside, he wrapped his jacket tightly around his chest and shoved his hands in his pockets.

Miss Celia's City House was dark when he returned. He used one of the keys Miss Celia handed out to her boarders and let himself in; then he took two steps at a time going up the stairs. After making the long walk to and from the hospital twice in the same evening, he was ready for bed.

The next morning, he came down for breakfast just as Mona and Bonnie were clearing the tables.

"Where's Kathryn?" he asked, grabbing a biscuit out of the basket before Mona could whisk it off the table.

"She left for school already. She said she'd be back around three."

"I'll be back around five. Tell her to let me know if she needs any help." Stan stuffed a bite of the freshly buttered biscuit into his mouth.

Mona grinned. "Okay."

He saw the gleam in her eye, but he chose to ignore the unspoken thoughts.

❦

Stan was late getting away from the prison, so when he arrived at Miss Celia's, dinner was in full swing. And so was the commotion in the dining room.

"Yuck!" one of the businesswomen said. "I don't like all this rich food."

"Me, neither," the man across from her replied. "What's wrong with normal food?"

Kathryn appeared at the door leading to the kitchen, a helpless, frantic expression on her face. His protective urge kicked into high gear. Stan crossed the dining room in three long strides, nudging her back into the kitchen.

"What's happening out there?" he asked softly as he stood at the kitchen door.

She looked up at him with fear. "Mutiny."

"I was afraid that might happen."

Kathryn planted her floured fist on her hip and glared at him. "I just wanted to do something really special for them."

That simple statement reminded him of all Jesus had done for humanity and how little His efforts were appreciated. But this was not the time to tell her that. Instead, he ushered her deeper into the kitchen to make sure no one else could hear.

"I have a simple suggestion," he said. "If you want to offer gourmet food, why don't you give them a choice?"

"That's sort of hard," she said. "And expensive."

"Maybe, but you won't have so many angry people, and you can get a feel for what they want."

"Yeah, but—"

She was interrupted by Mona, who pushed through the kitchen, a huge tray filled with uneaten portions of lamb. "They're mad," Mona said. "That one lady—the one with the big mouth—says she's not staying here next time she comes to New York."

Stan turned to Kathryn whose bottom lip was between her teeth. She needed to make a decision—quick.

"Just a minute," she said before running toward the dining room. She returned a minute later, looking dejected. "I promised them meatloaf tomorrow night. Aunt Celia's recipe."

"I'm sorry, Kathryn," Stan said.

"Yeah, me, too." Kathryn turned her back on him, grabbed a plate from the returned tray, and began scraping the contents into the garbage.

"Whoa, wait a minute," Stan said. "I know some people who would love that food."

"Your prisoners?" she asked sarcastically.

He nodded. "I'll have to bring a little extra for the guards, too."

Kathryn paused then nodded. "Yeah, I guess it's not a good idea to waste food when there are people who'll eat it, even if they are convicts."

Stan felt a thud in his chest.

❦

The snowstorm had returned by the next morning, only now there were no signs of it letting up. Stan carried sacks of food to the prison, garnering curious glances from people as he boarded the train. He smiled and nodded but didn't say a word. He was relieved that his favorite guard was on duty so he wouldn't get hassled about bringing in the food.

"Wow!" one of the men in his Bible study said.

"Someone can really cook."

As Stan left the prison, one of the guards told him the weather report was pretty harsh. "We're likely to get snowed in for a few days," he said.

The next morning, Stan glanced outside and saw a blanket of white snow hiding the sidewalks and a layer of ice with thick mounds of snow covering the street. He wasn't going anywhere.

"Good thing we ordered extra food," Kathryn said as he arrived at the breakfast table. "All roads in the city are impassable, so Mona and Bonnie can't come to work." She sniffled. "And my graduation ceremony has been put off until everything clears up."

"Have you called your aunt?" he asked.

Kathryn nodded. "She said she took physical therapy twice today, and it wore her out. I feel awful that I can't go see her."

"I'm sure she understands."

"She told me something else. Her physical therapist said she might need to go to a rehab facility for a few months, maybe even up to a year. She's not coming straight home from the hospital."

Stan thought he saw Kathryn's chin quiver. "Will you be able to stick around?"

"Of course. I wouldn't think of doing anything else.

Aunt Celia has made so many sacrifices for me, it would be wrong of me to leave."

"Sacrifices," Stan repeated.

"What?" Kathryn stopped and stared at him.

"Life is full of sacrifices."

"What are you talking about, Stan?"

Stan shrugged. "I was just thinking about how Mary and Joseph had to make so many sacrifices when God told them they'd be parents to the Christ child."

"Sounds more like an honor than a sacrifice to me."

"Yes, it was, and fortunately, they saw it that way. But think about it. They had to sacrifice their reputations when Mary became pregnant and they weren't yet married. Then they sacrificed their comfort to travel the distance. Another thing they sacrificed was dignity, parading in front of all those people who knew Mary was about to bear a child. Giving birth in a stable was another sacrifice." After a brief pause, he added, "And you know all the sacrifices Jesus made to witness to His followers."

Kathryn frowned and gulped. "Makes me feel petty."

"I wouldn't say that," Stan argued.

"Then what are you saying?" Kathryn asked.

"Just that the Lord understands and appreciates what it means for you to make sacrifices for the sake of others."

The remainder of the week, Kathryn stuck close to the menu her aunt had posted on the kitchen bulletin board. Although she'd accepted the boarders' simple tastes, Stan saw that her shoulders were sagging and her step had lost its bounce. The more he got to know her, the more he cared about her feelings.

"What's wrong, Kathryn?" he asked.

"Nothing."

"Come on. I can tell something's bugging you."

Her jaw tightened; then she spun around. "I called the head chef at the Don Cesar and told him it would be awhile before I could come down there."

"Was he okay with that?" Stan asked.

She rubbed her nose with the back of her hand. "He told me he couldn't wait very long."

"Sounds like he still wants you."

"That would be wishful thinking on my part. I told him to go ahead and bring in another apprentice. I have to stick around here until Aunt Celia returns."

"Trust that the Lord will provide what you're supposed to have." He knew this would be the perfect time for him to tell her about his past, but the words wouldn't come. His fear of her turning away from him overshadowed what he felt he needed to do.

"I'm working on it," she said as she turned back to her work.

⚉

Kathryn wasn't sure what had just happened, but she did know that whenever Stan was around, she felt a sense of peace, like everything would be okay, as he'd promised. His faith in God was strong and very evident. He made her want to learn more about God and why He allowed such things to happen. She'd always believed in God, and she knew about Jesus, but she never fully understood the depth of His love for humanity until Stan came along and made it seem so simple.

"You'll be okay, Kathryn," he said. "In fact, you're a very strong woman, just like your aunt."

She smiled. "Thanks."

Later that day, the streets were clear enough for Stan to go to work. "As soon as flights resume, I need to take a trip to Nashville," he told her.

A familiar dread washed over her as she remembered how her father had flitted in and out of her life.

⚉

Everything seemed to overshadow her graduation the

next day. Wasn't she supposed to be happy? When they were able to come back to work, Mona and Bonnie told her to enjoy her big day.

How could she enjoy it under the circumstances?

When Kathryn arrived at the institute, all the students and teaching chefs were chattering about how their families had struggled to change their plans. They made her painfully aware that she was the only one in the graduating class without someone there to witness the ceremony. She steeled herself against the pain.

At precisely five minutes before seven o'clock, the students lined up in alphabetical order, with Kathryn Anderson at the front of the line. She stood at the edge of the curtain, scanning the crowd, trying to imagine where Aunt Celia would have sat had she been there.

What? She blinked and leaned forward to get a better look. *What is* he *doing here?*

Stan Jarrett sat in the third row, dressed in a suit, and looking up at the stage expectantly. He looked more handsome than ever. If she didn't watch out, she could definitely fall in love with him.

Chapter 3

A momentary joy spread over Katherine as she studied the man who'd brought her comfort over the past several weeks. She wanted to talk to him, but there wasn't time.

After the final name was called, the administrator of the school invited all of the friends and family of the graduates to come up and sample some of the culinary delights. Kathryn hung out on the edge of the stage, watching as Stan made his way up.

Her heart raced as he came up to her. "Congratulations, Kathryn. Your aunt is very proud of you."

"I know she is. Did she put you up to coming?"

"No," he said firmly. "I came on my own. I've never been to a culinary school graduation before."

"And you've always wondered what it was like, right?"

He smiled back. "Something like that." He nodded toward the buffet. "And I'm dying to try that big brown, white, and beige thing in the center of the table."

"That big brown, white, and beige thing is a meringue. C'mon, let's go see what we can grab before the rest of the vultures polish it off."

She led him by the hand to the table. Several of her classmates looked at Stan and offered questioning glances, but no one said anything.

"Did you make any of this stuff?"

Kathryn nodded. "I helped with most of it, but I made the cheesecake by myself."

"Wow!" he said, after sampling the food on his plate. "This is incredible—especially the cheesecake. Can you cook all this?"

She nodded. "I hesitate to admit it, but yes."

"Why do you put it like that?"

"Aunt Celia's boarders, remember?"

"Oh yeah, the boarders. Well, you might want to fix them what they want, but if you ever get the urge to do something fancy, I'm all taste buds."

"That's nice to know. Thanks for the offer."

Being with Stan felt so natural—comfortable even. Stan was really a great guy, and she couldn't deny the tingle she felt when he looked at her with that twinkle in his eye and the mischievous grin.

"Hey, Kathryn," Chef Latour said as he gently placed his arm around her shoulder. "When do you leave for Florida?"

"I'm not going any time soon."

"What?" Chef Latour said with obvious dismay. "Don't tell me they changed their minds. Let me go call my friend and straighten this out. You will be the best chef in the East, and they should feel privileged you'd consider them."

"Oh, no, that's not it."

Chef Latour glanced at Stan with an accusing glare. "Do you have something to do with this?"

"No, I—"

"It's my aunt," Kathryn blurted. "She fell and has to stay in the hospital."

A look of remorse crossed Chef Latour's face. "Oh my, I'm so sorry. If there's anything I can do, please let me know."

After he left, Stan leaned over and whispered, "Wanna go home?"

Kathryn inhaled, allowing her senses to experience his close proximity and clean scent. She nodded.

"Why don't we walk to the next station?" she said.

"I need to get rid of some of this energy."

"If you can handle the cold, then I certainly can." He gently placed his arm around her shoulder, and she allowed herself to snuggle into his warmth.

Conversation between them felt natural. He asked questions about her plans for the future, and she admitted she wasn't sure now. Then she turned the questions back to him.

"Why are you involved in the prison ministry?" she asked.

She felt him tense, but after a few seconds, he relaxed a little. "This is something I feel called to do."

"Wouldn't you reach more people if you became a pulpit preacher?"

"I'm not sure. I talk to a lot of people in jail. If I can bring comfort to hurting people and let them know where they can spend eternity, I feel like I need to continue doing that."

"Those people have done crimes, though. Shouldn't they suffer for the pain they've caused others?"

"Oh, trust me, Kathryn, they're suffering plenty."

"You sound like you feel sorry for them."

"Some of them might even be innocent."

"Come on, Stan. You can't be that naive. People don't get thrown in jail if they've never committed a crime."

"Some do," he argued.

"I don't believe that for a minute."

They walked in silence the rest of the way to Miss Celia's City House. Kathryn knew something had changed between them during the conversation, but she couldn't put her finger on exactly what.

⚬⚬⚬

As they arrived at the boardinghouse, Stan couldn't think of a reason to keep her from going up to her room, although he wanted to be with her just a little longer.

She took one step up, turned, and smiled. "Thanks for coming to the ceremony, Stan. That was very sweet of you."

"I wouldn't have missed it for anything."

Their gazes locked for several seconds before Kathryn turned and ran up the stairs. He felt an odd sensation burning in his gut as she disappeared behind the upstairs wall.

The next morning, Stan stopped off to see Miss Celia on his way to work. She'd just finished breakfast and was wrestling with a newspaper.

"This thing's so big, I almost can't read it anymore," she grumbled.

"Well, good morning to you, too, Miss Celia."

146

"Sorry." She folded the paper and put it down on the bed beside her. "It's just so frustrating to be in this bed while the whole world is out there moving around."

"I can imagine."

She snorted. "I s'pose it's sort of like how your prisoners feel most days."

"Yes, except they can walk and move around."

"This is worse, huh?" she said. "I just might have to break out of this prison if the doctor doesn't release me soon."

"You can't do that, Miss Celia. I was just kidding."

"I know you were. So how's it going with my niece?"

"She seems to be okay," he said.

"Uh-huh. Tell me another good one. C'mon, Stan. I've known you for a while. I see that hangdog expression you've had since you first walked in here. You can tell me what's on your mind."

He shrugged. "I don't know for sure myself, so how can I tell you? Besides, it's almost time for your therapy, and I have a bunch of inmates waiting to hear the rest of Matthew. I'm reading the New Testament to my small group."

"The whole New Testament?"

"Yes. I just hope I don't get transferred before I'm finished."

"That'll take you forever, but that's okay with me. I like having you here."

"And I like being here."

Stan had gotten almost to the door when she called out his name. He quickly turned and faced her.

"You might want to start thinking of a way to let Kathryn know about your incarceration. I'd love to see the two of you get to know each other better, and she needs honesty."

Miss Celia could see right through him. But after all she'd been through, how could he tell Kathryn he'd spent nearly three months as an inmate?

"I'll look for an opening in conversation," he said.

"Just don't wait too long," Miss Celia advised.

He pursed his lips, offered a crisp nod, then left.

Stan knew he would have been bitter had the Lord not come into his life when he hit rock bottom. He would still be in jail had the robber for whom Stan was mistaken not held up another convenience store. Although he wouldn't wish his experience on anyone, Stan knew the Lord had used it for overall good.

He reflected on how he'd begun his relationship with the Lord. When the group of men from the prison ministry had left Bibles, he'd picked one up and carried it back to his cell because there wasn't anything better to do. As he read and reread the promises of the Lord, Stan's view of life had gradually changed. By the time he was released, he possessed a whole different attitude and purpose for living, and he was eager to serve the Lord. His prayers had been answered, and he'd been given the opportunity through Prison Fellowship.

The train ride to the prison was long, so he had time to think about how to tell Kathryn about his past. But no matter what he said, he knew it would hit her with a jolt and she would put up the shield he'd seen so many times.

After arriving at the prison, he stepped into the first room, took off his belt and shoelaces, and waited for his locker assignment for his personal belongings. He knew the drill. Nothing was allowed on the other side that would enable a prisoner to escape, hurt someone, or commit suicide.

The group waited for him in the visitation area. One of the prisoners had been coming for weeks, while the others were newer and more skeptical. He kept his personal greetings low-key. In prison, trust was one gift that had to be earned—and that often took much longer than in the outside world.

He finished reading the book of Matthew and asked the men if they had any questions. For a while, it appeared no one would say a word, but then one of the newcomers lifted his hand.

"Yes, Rodney?" Stan said. "You have a question?"

"Why didn't Jesus just wipe out all those people who were mocking him? Maybe people would have listened. He didn't have to die like that."

Stan smiled. He'd heard that question before. "One thing I've learned is that God doesn't always take the easy way out. In fact, what he did for mankind by allowing Jesus to be crucified was probably more difficult than anything any of us will have to face."

Another of the prisoners snorted, stuck out his legs in front of him, and slouched down in his seat as he folded his arms, virtually shutting out the world around him. "I don't know about that, man. This place can be pretty rough."

"Yes, I know," Stan agreed. "But imagine how much worse it would be if you had guards taunting you with sticks and then having to walk to your death, carrying a heavy cross, knowing you were about to be nailed to it and left there to die."

"Yeah, that's extreme," the inmate said. "But I'm like Rodney. I don't see why Jesus didn't just perform a miracle and get down from that cross."

"I think the answers to your questions will become clearer as we go deeper into the New Testament."

Later that night, Stan shared the questions with Kathryn. She nodded.

"I've often wondered the same thing," she said. "But then I've also wondered why Adam and Eve could have been so foolish to blatantly disobey God, when they had everything handed to them that they could possibly want."

Stan grinned. "I guess they were acting like spoiled children in the Garden of Eden."

"Sure appears that way," Kathryn said. "And now we all have to suffer."

She'd just given him another opportunity to tell her about his past. He cleared his throat, opened his mouth, and then watched her eyes light up.

"Oh, I forgot to tell you," she said with excitement. "I had some Key limes shipped up from Florida, and I made you a pie this afternoon."

He felt as if someone had knocked the wind out of him. "You're very sweet, Kathryn."

He watched her blush, which left his pulse racing. "I like doing things for you, Stan," she said softly.

Each day, he vowed to discuss his past with Kathryn, but something always came up. Miss Celia became more and more stern with him, showing her disapproval over his silence. He wanted to do the right thing—and he fully intended to. Someday.

"Christmas is coming soon, Miss Celia," he reminded her during one of his daily visits.

"Yeah, and all I want from you is for you to tell my niece about what you went through."

Now he had no choice. "Okay. I'll do it."

"Good boy."

Later that night, after Mona and Bonnie left, Stan joined Kathryn in the kitchen. "Would you like to talk for a little while before bedtime?" he asked.

She nodded, her eyes wide, her smile wider. Stan took a step closer to her. She was particularly beautiful when she smiled, and her kindness touched his heart in a way nothing else could. Suddenly, he felt an overwhelming urge to kiss her.

※

Kathryn followed him to the sitting room then stopped when he turned toward her. He slowly reached out, took her hand, and kissed the back of her fingers, leaving her senses heightened at the point of contact. There was no doubt she was falling in love with him, and there was nothing she could do to stop it.

"Kathryn," he whispered softly, as he pulled her into his arms. She tilted her face up to his and slowly melted into his embrace, knowing she was about to be kissed.

Chapter 4

As Stan's lips found hers, Kathryn let out a sigh. His kiss was tender—just like the man. He quickly pulled away from the kiss, which had rendered her incapable of speaking. He led her to the loveseat by the window.

Stan sat in silence for a few moments before he shook his head. "I'm sorry if I upset you, Kathryn."

A chuckle escaped her throat, and she found her voice. "You didn't upset me. I liked it."

"So did I. Very much." He glanced away then turned back to her. "What are you thinking?"

"Nothing."

"Just empty thoughts?"

Kathryn started to nod, but instead, she turned and looked him in the eye. "No. It's just that. . ."

How could she tell him he'd turned her entire world upside down? He totally confused her and made her wish she'd never met him, yet she wanted to be near him all the time.

"Just that *what?*" he asked slowly.

"Nothing," she replied.

As quickly as his smile appeared, it left, and he removed his hands from hers. "We need to move slowly."

Her heart fell. "You're right."

He sat and stared at his steepled hands as if he'd never seen them before. Kathryn's stomach let out a loud rumble.

"Still hungry?" he asked, his voice sounding hoarse.

"No. Just a little nervous. Are you okay?"

Kathryn held her breath as he gazed deeply into her eyes once again. The tugging sensation at her heart was more noticeable than before the kiss. In a way, she regretted it, but the feeling was so nice, she wouldn't have traded it for anything. Conflicting emotions swelled inside her.

"You look like the nervous one," he replied. "Why don't we call it a night? We both have some thinking to do."

The warmth of his lips on hers lingered as she left Stan alone. She knew he didn't want to part ways any more than she did, but it was for their own good. He'd brought her to her senses and let her know without words that his mission was stronger than anything between them.

As she undressed and got ready for bed, all Kathryn could think about was how wonderful and natural it felt to kiss and be kissed by Stan. Kathryn slipped beneath the covers and hunkered down with her head on the soft, down pillow. She shut her eyes and asked God to give her wisdom and the ability to understand what was going on in her life. More things than she could count had cropped up, confusing her and making her wonder if she'd ever accomplish her goal.

She must have fallen asleep soon after she ended her prayer, because when she opened her eyes and blinked, it was light outside. One quick glance at her alarm clock let her know she'd overslept.

Swinging her legs over the side of the bed, Kathryn rubbed her eyes. She quickly got up, washed her face, brushed her teeth, dressed, and flew down to the kitchen, where Bonnie was scurrying back and forth between the dining room and kitchen. Glancing around the crowded dining room, she noticed one person who wasn't there.

"Where's Stan?"

"He had to go back to Nashville," Bonnie said over her shoulder before disappearing behind the swinging kitchen door.

Kathryn was right on her heels. "What?"

"His supervisor with the ministry called and said he needed to come back. They were shorthanded, and they needed him."

Kathryn felt a quick thud in her chest as that old resentment crept up and caught her off guard. "Well, good," she said sarcastically. "Now maybe we can get some work done."

Bonnie opened her mouth, but then quickly closed it and shook her head. Good thing, too. Kathryn didn't feel like listening to excuses or sympathetic apologies.

"I need to get moving," Kathryn said as she scurried around the kitchen.

Bonnie followed close behind.

When the delivery people came half an hour later, Kathryn had to check the order. Bonnie busied herself by getting lunch ready for the boarders and local businesspeople who came during the week.

After lunch cleanup, Kathryn shoved her arms in her coat. "I need to go see Aunt Celia for a little while. I'll be back in an hour or two."

"Take your time," Bonnie said, then winked and

offered an understanding smile.

Kathryn forced herself to smile back, even though she felt overwhelmed at the moment. She was being thrown so many curveballs lately, and she wasn't sure what to do with them all.

Aunt Celia didn't act the least bit surprised when she told her about Stan leaving. "That's something you'll have to accept about him."

"I know, but. . ."

Kathryn wasn't sure how to say what she felt about Stan. But when she glanced up at her aunt, she had a feeling she didn't have to say anything. Aunt Celia was a smart woman.

Finally, after a moment of silence, Aunt Celia sighed. "All this therapy's wearing me out. I barely have time to read my Bible."

"I wish there was something I could do," Kathryn said.

"I know, sweetheart. But this is only temporary."

"Is there any way you'll be able to come home for Christmas?" Kathryn asked.

Aunt Celia cleared her throat. "I'm working on it. It's still a couple weeks away."

"Want me to talk to the doctors?"

"It's my physical therapist who's holding things up.

He's afraid I'll do something stupid and fall again."

"What if I promise to keep an eye on you and not let you do anything risky?"

"That might work," she said with a chuckle. "Someone needs to keep an eye on me, I s'pose."

"I need to get back. Call me later, okay?"

Kathryn had made it to the door when her aunt's voice made her pause. "I'm sorry about Stan."

"Hey, Stan has a job to do. It's no big deal."

"When change comes in life, it only means that the Lord has something else in store for us. You might not see it right away, but it's generally better than anything we could have planned."

As Kathryn left the hospital, she thought about that last comment. She wished she had that kind of faith.

※※

Two weeks later, Miss Celia was waiting at her hospital room door, ready to go home. "I thought you'd never get here," she told Kathryn. "Let's go!"

Chapter 5

I'm sure he'd be here if he could," Aunt Celia said as Kathryn wheeled her up the ramp Stan had made and to the front door. Kathryn had talked the physical therapist into releasing her aunt for a few days. It was Christmas Eve, and most of the boarders had gone home to be with their own families. Only a few lonely people stayed behind. "Hold on for a minute, dear. Let me catch my breath before we go inside. It's been a long time."

"I understand," Kathryn said. "This must be hard for you."

"Not hard, exactly. Just overwhelming. I miss being here more than you can ever imagine."

Once they were inside the house, the boarders who were still there greeted them and then went to their own rooms. Aunt Celia let out a long sigh.

"I love this place, but I know I can't hold onto it forever."

"What are you talking about?" Kathryn said, suddenly feeling a tightening in her abdomen. She couldn't fathom Aunt Celia not having her boardinghouse. "You'll be up and around in no time. Your physical therapist even told me you were doing great and should expect a full recovery."

With sadness in her eyes, Aunt Celia studied Kathryn. "I've worked hard all my life. I've had quite a bit of time to think lately, and I might be ready for something different."

Kathryn felt the urge to change the subject. "Let's go into the kitchen and see if Mona and Bonnie left you a plate."

After they sat down to reheated leftovers, Aunt Celia said the blessing then turned to Kathryn. "I sure do wish Stan could be here."

"Me, too," Kathryn murmured so softly she wasn't sure her aunt could hear.

After they ate dinner, mostly in silence, Kathryn wheeled her aunt to the bedroom she'd prepared downstairs. "If you need me, just ring this," she said, pointing to the bell on the nightstand.

Aunt Celia chuckled. "You're a dear, but you're also a glutton for punishment."

The next morning was Christmas, so Kathryn quickly gathered all the gifts she'd stored in her closet. They were all small things that her aunt could use in the rehab center, like a coin purse to keep her change for the vending machines, a lap robe, a lightweight sweater that she could easily pull on and off, and some paperback novels Kathryn knew she enjoyed.

"You shouldn't have," Aunt Celia said as she opened the last of her gifts. "You did way too much for me. It's enough that you're running this place while I'm laid up."

"I really wanted to do it," Kathryn replied, thrilled her aunt liked everything.

"I have something for you, too," Aunt Celia said. She pulled out the Bible that once belonged to her mother, Kathryn's grandmother. "She'd want you to have this, I'm sure."

Kathryn opened the Bible and lingered on the page with the family tree. She felt her throat constrict as tears welled in her eyes.

"Dad's name is in here," she said, her voice shaking.

"Yes, so it is," Aunt Celia said softly. "I'm just sorry he never stuck around long enough to listen to our mother share her faith."

"I've always wondered about that. How did Dad miss the wonderful message of God's love?"

Aunt Celia took Kathryn's hand and held it. "This is probably a good time to share some things with you."

Kathryn sat and listened to the story of her wanderlust father, who left home when he was still in his teens. He always thought there was something better out there, and he didn't want to miss out on anything—especially a chance to grab his fortune. She hadn't seen him in years.

"Too bad he was such a liar," Kathryn said.

Aunt Celia sighed and shook her head. "I don't think he started out that way. He just got caught up in the excitement of latching onto a better life, and he had a lapse in judgment."

"A lapse that destroyed his family," Kathryn reminded her.

Aunt Celia leveled her with a serious look. "No, Kathryn. It did injure the family, but it didn't destroy us. You and I still have each other, and we have the love of Christ. I pray every day for your mother, but that's all we can do. Your father may change one of these days, but you have to move forward, even if he doesn't."

Kathryn slowly nodded. "Yes, you're right, Aunt Celia. And I'm thankful to have you."

"Not any more thankful than I am to have you.

Being here right now is the best Christmas present I could possibly have."

"Time to get breakfast ready for the lonely boarders," Kathryn said. "I picked up a few gifts for them."

⁂

"We're doing everything we can," Reverend Martin said when Stan expressed his desire to return to New York right after Christmas. "It's just that we're so short-handed with the flu going around and everyone wanting time with their families."

"I understand," Stan replied. And he did.

It was mid-January before he managed to go back to New York. He was thankful for the flexibility in his ministry, but it was time to settle down.

Stan's pulse quickened at the sight of Kathryn as she entered the front door and breezed past him, heading for the kitchen. She was a woman on a mission. He liked that about her. Nothing about Kathryn was halfway.

"How's your aunt?" he asked. "Did she have a nice Christmas?"

Kathryn nodded. "It was pleasant. I just wish she could have stayed longer."

Kathryn stood several feet from him, appearing to be intentionally keeping her distance. "I wish I could've been here," he said, feeling awkward.

"Aunt Celia would have like that."

"How about you?" he asked.

Her lower lip trembled as she stared at her hands and then looked up at him. "To be honest, I'm not sure."

Her comment hit him like a ton of bricks. He gulped. "Thanks for being honest, Kathryn."

Her opinion mattered more than he wanted it to. He was falling in love with her, a disaster in the making.

"I have to start dinner, Stan," she said as she backed away from him and slid out of the room, leaving him alone. He felt like the floor beneath him might open up and swallow him alive.

He finally went up to his room to prepare the lesson for the next day. But, no matter how hard he tried to focus on his work, his conversation with Kathryn kept creeping into his head, forcing him to give up and rely solely on prayer.

Squeezing his eyes shut, he begged for some direction that would knock him upside the head. "Otherwise, Lord, I might miss what you want for me. Amen."

The aroma of spices and seasonings wafted up to him, drawing him back down a couple of hours later.

Stan entered the dining room in time to hear more grumbling among the boarders. He instantly felt the urge to protect her. Although he managed to quiet them for now, he suspected they'd pick up where they left off after he was gone.

He bowed his head and said a prayer of thanksgiving for any food he was fortunate to have.

Kathryn suddenly appeared at the door, holding a platter of some fancy stuffed bird. Stan held his breath, waiting for someone to make a wisecrack, but then Mona was right behind her with a very large meatloaf, sliced and doused with ketchup, just like the other boarders liked it.

"We're giving you a choice," Kathryn announced. "You can have the traditional boardinghouse food, or you can have something different." She looked around the room then added, "Something special."

Stan raised his hand, which Kathryn immediately acknowledged. "May I have some of both?"

Taking his lead, the other boarders requested both. Stan's earlier indignation faded, and he was grateful for the softening of the boarders.

People literally ate double their usual amount. Kathryn stood around and observed in amazement while Stan watched her. He loved seeing her happy, knowing she'd brought something good into the lives of these people. Her earlier dour expression had softened, which lifted his heart.

After the rest of the boarders had gone to their rooms, Stan stood. He picked up his own plate and stacked it with the others at his table. When he appeared at the kitchen door, Kathryn met him and tried to take the stack from him.

"No," he said as he turned away, preventing her from grabbing the plates. "I'm helping clean up."

"You don't need to do that," she said, avoiding his gaze.

"I've already told you before, I like doing this."

Kathryn paused then said, "Okay, suit yourself. Just put 'em in the sink." She left him and went out to the dining room to gather up some more of the dirty dinnerware.

Stan had already begun loading the dishwasher when she came back. "The sink was full," he explained.

Without saying a word, she put her stack on the counter and went back for more. Mona had gone home for the day, so that left Bonnie as the only hired help there. Stan knew if he didn't help, Kathryn would still be cleaning long after Bonnie went home. He might be a slow, but at least they could make progress a little faster.

When they finished, Kathryn wiped her hands on a towel. "Thanks again, Stan. I wish you didn't feel like you had to do that, but I really appreciate it."

"I don't feel like I have to," he replied. "I truly like doing it."

"What's your game, Stan?"

"Game?"

Her forehead crinkled. "You waltz in and out of here like nothing else matters but your prisoners. I don't get it."

"Please, Kathryn, let me explain, okay?"

"Not tonight, Stan. I have a lot on my mind."

He knew now wasn't the right time to press. "Okay, fine, Kathryn, but we do need to talk."

He turned to go up to his room and hesitated as he reached the door.

"Stan?"

Spinning on his heel, he looked at her.

"Do you really think they liked dinner? The boarders, I mean."

"They cleaned their plates, didn't they?"

She offered a hint of a smile, which gave him a tiny speck of hope. "G'night, Stan."

"Good night, Kathryn. Get some rest."

As he watched Kathryn ascend the stairs, Stan knew he'd have no peace until he told her everything. First thing tomorrow.

After breakfast the next morning, Kathryn cast curious glances his way. Finally, she said, "Aren't you supposed to be working?"

"We need to talk."

"Okay," she said, her voice cracking. "Let me finish here."

Once the breakfast dishes had been washed and put away, she turned to him. "You wanted to talk, so talk."

He joined her at the kitchen table. They sat in silence until Stan knew he had to speak. "Okay, this is hard, but I guess I'd better speak my mind. I really like you, Kathryn. I've never felt this way about a woman before."

She managed a shaky grin as she looked him in the eye, her guard not quite as high. "I have a confession to make."

"A confession?"

Kathryn opened her mouth then shook her head. "Nothing. It doesn't matter. Go on. So you were saying you never felt this way before?"

"Yes. But. . ."

"Here it comes," she said, the shield returning. "There's always a *but*."

"Unfortunately, my ministry is based in Nashville. I'm part of a loan program of prison ministers. Until recently, I've been more than happy to travel. But things have changed. I've applied for a job working directly for the prison here in New York, but there's no guarantee it'll come through."

"It probably won't come through," she said sarcastically.

The defeat he heard in her voice broke his heart. "Kathryn," he began as he reached for her hand.

"Don't," she said. "I don't want to hear any more."

"Things would have been much simpler if we'd met under different circumstances. My life is such a mess."

She looked at him straight on, defiance evident in her eyes. "I'm the one who's a mess. Your life is the one with meaning. I bet you've always known exactly where you were going in your life, haven't you?"

Chapter 6

The sudden look of anguish in his eyes tore at her heart. Had she been too hard on him?

"No, not really," he said. "There's something you should know about me."

"And that is?"

"It's something I did. . .or, rather, didn't do in my past."

"I'm not in the mood to play games, Stan. Just spit it out."

She watched him swallow hard before leveling her with a gaze that was downright scary. He looked like a completely different person.

"I spent three months in prison," he blurted as he looked away, "for a crime I didn't commit."

"You what?" she asked. She felt her body stiffen.

Surely she'd heard wrong.

"A few years ago, I was working a job I didn't care for, repairing computers in an electronics store. I'd been trying to find something else to do with my life, and I confided in one of the other techs about it. He said he thought I was nuts because we made decent money and quite a few people had been getting laid off. Our jobs were secure, but that didn't affect how I felt about my job."

"How did that get you thrown in jail?" Kathryn asked as she edged away from him.

"I thought he'd forgotten about our talk, but obviously he hadn't. The local convenience store was robbed several weeks later, and when they put the guy's image from the store security videotape on TV, the tech at work thought the robber looked like me. He called the hotline and told them I wasn't happy with my job and that he thought I was the guy who robbed the convenience store."

"How did that get you sent to jail? Job dissatisfaction isn't a crime." She studied him before adding, "And from what I've seen, those videotapes aren't the best in the world. Lots of people have similar features to yours." *But none that came together so well*, she thought.

"No, but when the police came to interview me at

work, I wasn't exactly polite about it."

"Did you resist arrest?"

"No," he said with a sardonic chuckle. "In fact, they didn't even arrest me right away. I told them they were barking up the wrong tree, but they insisted I answer their questions. I told them to get out. They told me I had no choice but to cooperate, and eventually, the argument escalated until my boss told me to go home and not to come back."

"That's awful," Kathryn said. "But I don't understand why you didn't cooperate from the beginning. That doesn't sound like you."

"Maybe not now, but back then I had a chip on my shoulder. Until I had a personal relationship with the Lord, I wasn't the most agreeable guy around."

This was news Kathryn needed to pay attention to. From her personal experience, people didn't change. They only hid the truth. At such deception, her father had been the best she'd ever seen—that is, until now.

"They made me go to a lineup," he continued, "and the manager of the convenience store picked me, of all people. Then they hauled me off to jail."

"You said you were only there for three months. That doesn't seem long for armed robbery." Kathryn continued to edge farther away from him.

"The guy who'd actually robbed the store did it again. This time, he was sloppy and got caught. When it came out that he'd robbed the one I'd been accused of, all charges were dropped."

"Did you try to get your old job back?"

"No," he said. "While I was in prison, I developed an interest in the ministry. This might sound strange to you, but I saw that time in prison as a message to change my life. I noticed firsthand that when people have committed a crime and they're caught, they tend to be more open to hearing the gospel."

"That does seem strange. I would have thought the opposite." Kathryn now felt numb. She wasn't sure if she should believe him, but she did know she needed to stay as far away from him as she could get.

"In some people, you'll see extreme bitterness. But in others, once they have nothing to do but think about how they've hurt other people and messed up their own lives, they want to do something to change things. Their vulnerabilities have been exposed, so they tend to go one way or another."

"So that's how you got into the prison ministry, huh?"

"Yep. That's it in a nutshell."

Kathryn hated secrets. And now that she'd learned

Stan's secret, she felt betrayed not only by him but by herself. She'd allowed herself to feel something for this man—this ex-con.

Silence fell between them as she mentally processed what he'd told her. Finally, he stood and nodded. "Guess I'd better get on to my room. I have to prepare for tomorrow."

She watched him leave the room, his head hanging. Her limbs felt numb, so she waited several minutes before trying to stand.

Stan figured it was a mistake to blurt it all out so fast, but once he'd gotten started, he couldn't seem to stop. Okay, so now the ball was in Kathryn's court. He'd have to give her time to sort through all he'd told her. Kathryn obviously didn't understand what he'd gone through, and he had to admit, neither did he. He'd forgiven the man who'd been responsible for his being in jail, but the memories hadn't been as easily erased from his mind.

Flashbacks kept him from sleeping as they haunted him all night. He went down to breakfast feeling like a beaten man. Kathryn did a double take when she saw him, but she didn't give him even a hint of a smile.

On the way to the prison, he stopped off and saw Miss Celia. "Hey, Stan, you look rough." She narrowed her focus then slowly shook her head. "You told Kathryn, didn't you?"

"Afraid so," he replied. "And now I know it was a mistake. I should have waited."

"Did you tell her all the details?"

"As much as I could."

"Then don't worry about it."

He huffed. "That's easy for you to say, Miss Celia. She loves you no matter what."

"Well, that might be so, but it has nothing to do with the two of you."

"I know." He leaned over and gave her a quick peck on the cheek. "Gotta run. The men are waiting to hear more about Jesus."

"How's the New Testament coming along?" she asked.

"Good. They've asked some thought-provoking questions."

"Yeah," she said. "And I bet some of them are designed to trip you up."

"I'm sure."

"Hold on a minute, Stan. I want you to tell me something."

Thinking Miss Celia had a question about his ministry, he stepped back into the room. "Okay, whatever you want to know."

"Do you love my niece?"

He froze in place. That simple question—those five words—had stunned him.

"Uh. . ." He glanced down at his feet. "Yes, I do, Miss Celia."

"Well, you better figure out how to let her know that, too. I can only stall her so long."

"Stall her? I don't want you to do that."

Miss Celia offered one of her I-know-what-I'm-doing lopsided grins. "Looks to me like you might need some help."

"I appreciate the offer, but I think we should let the Lord work through this without any interference."

A contrite expression instantly formed on her face. She nodded. "Yes, you're absolutely right. I'll behave."

He offered a grin and a wave. "Thanks for the offer, though. It's very sweet of you."

"Sweet?" she said with a cackle. "That's a new one." She paused for a second before looking coyly up at him. "You think I'm sweet?"

"Yes," he replied. "You're one of the sweetest people I've ever met."

Her eyes misted over. "You're a good boy, Stan. Most people would have come out of your situation with hardened hearts. But you've taken lemons and made lemonade. I wish more people were like you."

"Don't go getting all mushy on me, Miss Celia. You know that makes me uncomfortable."

She giggled. "It's fun making a man squirm."

"You're too much," he said as he left the room.

About halfway through the Bible study with the inmates, he was interrupted by one of the men who'd attended since the beginning but hadn't opened his mouth until now.

"Hey, Rev, I got a question for you," the man said, as he folded his arms over his chest and narrowed his eyes.

"What's that, George?"

"You got something else on your mind?" He shook his head and smirked. "Looks like you might be thinkin' about some woman or somethin'."

Might as well be honest. These guys would see right through him.

"Yeah, afraid so."

All the men hooted and made cat sounds. "We knew it. You can't hide nothin' from the boys."

"Okay, so now that you're on to me, would you mind praying for me?" he asked.

They all exchanged glances then nodded. George spoke up. "Ya gotta tell us exactly what to pray for, man, or we won't know what to say to God."

Chapter 7

S tan told them just enough to get them all smiling then said he really needed to go. "Hey, man, you need to let the lady know how you feel," George said. "Women like stuff like that."

"Thanks, George. I'll do my best."

His cell phone rang the second he got it back from the prison guards. "We need you back in Nashville, Stan."

A knot formed in his chest. "What happened?"

"Some of the prisoners got a little rowdy, and now Joe's in the hospital."

"I'll be there as soon as I can."

Stan had always known he was in a high-risk profession, but this was the first time he'd personally known someone who'd gotten hurt. He said a prayer for his friend Joe and then went inside to let Kathryn know he was leaving again.

"Just let us know when we need to get your room ready again," she said without any sign of emotion.

***

Kathryn's conviction had now officially been reinforced. She never should have let her guard down—not even a smidgen. Stan wasn't any better than her father; in fact, he may have been worse. Her father had never claimed to be a godly man.

Why Aunt Celia had insisted on her keeping a room for Stan, Kathryn couldn't imagine. They had a waiting list of boarders. But she'd learned early on that arguing with Aunt Celia wouldn't do her a bit of good.

Each time Stan showed up over the next several months, Kathryn forced herself to keep her distance. Finally, autumn came and went, and Aunt Celia was making sounds about coming home before Christmas— permanently. The physical therapist at the rehab center was aggressively pushing her to work hard.

A whole year had passed since Aunt Celia's fall. Stan continued to travel back and forth between New York and Nashville.

"We have some things to discuss," Aunt Celia said a week before she was due to go home.

"I need to get a downstairs room ready for you."

"That's great, but my room is the least of my concerns. I've been doing quite a bit of thinking." She glanced down then added, "About the City House."

"Not about *giving up* the City House, I hope," Kathryn replied.

"Yes, dear, that's exactly what I want to discuss. I've had some offers, and I don't want to let an opportunity get away."

Kathryn felt that sick feeling as she let herself imagine her aunt retiring. She couldn't look her in the eye.

"Have you been reading your Bible, Kathryn?"

"Not only have I been reading my Bible, you'll be pleased to know I've been going to your church. Everyone wants to stop by when you get home."

"All my friends at church are such dears," Aunt Celia said. "They've been visiting and bringing me presents."

Kathryn chuckled. "Don't expect to keep getting all those presents after you get home."

"I hope they don't bring me anything because, to be honest with you, it's embarrassing. I never know what to say."

✥

Stan was waiting for Kathryn when she returned to the

boardinghouse. "Your room's ready," she said flatly.

"Can we talk?"

She shrugged. "About what?"

He looked at her then sighed. "Never mind. You don't look like you're in the mood for a chat—at least not with me."

Kathryn wished she didn't feel that familiar tug at her heart when he looked at her like that. Finally, she conceded. "Maybe later, okay?"

A flicker of hope appeared in his eyes. "Great. Tonight?"

"Fine. Tonight after dinner."

They had the routine down from before. Eat dinner, gather and wash dishes, and head to the sitting room. Kathryn was there first, and she started the conversation.

"Aunt Celia is coming home soon, and she's talking about selling this place."

"When?" Stan said.

"Day after tomorrow," Kathryn replied.

"And she wants to sell this place?"

Miss Celia had discussed several options she'd been considering since her accident, and although he'd miss having this wonderful place to stay, he thought she might be right—maybe it was time to move on to the next phase of her life. She needed a change.

Kathryn looked at him and nodded. Her expression was rigid. Determined. Rehearsed.

"Tell you what, Kathryn," he said. "I'll tell the guys at the prison you need me here, and I'll stick around to make sure everything's okay when she returns."

He knew he'd said the wrong thing the second he saw her jaw tighten even more. "I don't need you to do that. I'm perfectly capable—"

"I know you're capable, but I want to be here. Miss Celia has done so much for me, I can't imagine not helping at least a little."

He watched as she thought it over, now realizing he hadn't given her much choice. "Okay, I guess that would be all right. She'll probably like it."

"Do we need to get a downstairs room ready?" he asked. "She's always had the room on the second floor, but that won't work. At least not yet. It might be a while before she can navigate the stairs."

Kathryn groaned. "I'll have to do some shuffling of guests. There's nothing available on the main floor."

"I thought Gus was leaving."

"Not for another week," Kathryn said. "But his room would be perfect. I'll talk to him in the morning after breakfast."

"You'd better get some rest," Stan advised. "You'll need it. I have a feeling you'll be very busy while she's here."

She sighed. "No doubt."

As Kathryn ascended the stairs, he saw her shoulders sag, the weight of the world dragging her down. He wished he could say or do something to make her feel better, but he knew from experience there were just some things that she had to handle on her own.

❧

Kathryn shut her bedroom door behind her before slumping into the chair by the door. She'd had her whole life planned, but nothing was turning out right. To top it off, she felt guilty for dreading the time Aunt Celia would be home.

The more she thought about everything, the more confused she got. Her head ached, and she felt the weight on her shoulders as burdens kept piling on, brick by brick.

With a heavy sigh, Kathryn stood and got ready for bed. After crawling beneath the covers, she rummaged around and found her Bible, then settled back on her propped up pillows.

Aunt Celia had called and mentioned something about the book of Luke, chapter twenty-three, verses forty through forty-one. Kathryn found the verses.

After reading the Scripture ahead of it, she understood that this was where Jesus was talking to the criminals when he'd been nailed to the cross. After one of them had hurled insults, the other said, " 'Don't you fear God,' he said, 'since you are under the same sentence? . . . For we are getting what our deeds deserve. But this man has done nothing wrong.' "

Kathryn turned the Bible upside down on her comforter, shut her eyes, and thought about how this verse applied to her life. She knew Jesus was the perfect example of how people should be; her aunt had taught her that early in life. Aunt Celia was the wisest woman she knew, and she was also loving in a totally unconditional way. She never expected anything in return from anyone, including her own brother.

After being disappointed time after time by her parents, Kathryn had a difficult time trusting anyone—except Aunt Celia, who'd never let her down. Her father had lied his way through everything with her and her mother, and her mother had gotten into community theater as a hobby. When she'd been discovered by the man who opened the tiny dinner theater on the edge of town, she jumped at the chance to get paid and call herself a professional actress. From then on, she left Kathryn home alone most nights.

The summers she spent with Aunt Celia were the only times Kathryn felt as though someone cared enough about her to give her the attention she needed. Her aunt always sent her home with recipes, which Kathryn then embellished. The first positive words out of her mother's mouth were, "Wow, girl, you cook like the chefs in the fine restaurants of New York."

That set Kathryn to thinking about a future in the restaurant business. If she could do this on her own without any training, she wondered what she could do if she had the best teachers in the world.

After high school, she remained at home while she went to the community college and got a liberal arts degree, worked retail, and saved her money for her goal.

Aunt Celia had been delighted and encouraged her to follow her dream. Even her mother thought it sounded exciting.

So Kathryn embarked on a journey that she assumed would be filled with obstacles, but she'd determined to overcome them. And she had. Until now.

All the what-ifs fluttered through her mind. What if she never had an opportunity to work with a great chef, like the one at the Don Cesar? What if Aunt Celia needed more from her than she could give? What if Stan was right about God's plan?

Squeezing her eyes shut, she chewed on her bottom lip as she silently prayed.

Lord, thank You so much for the blessing of Aunt Celia. She has been my protector and anchor during troubled times. And thank You for the past three years and allowing me to complete the culinary program. That was truly a blessing. I'm coming to You with a heaviness on my heart and have no idea what to do with my life. Please give me some direction and guidance so I don't keep digging deeper into frustration. And Lord, while you're at it, I pray that You'll enlighten me and give me a peace about whatever relationship You want me to have with Stan. My attraction to him frightens me, and I know that's not what You want. I know You don't want me making deals with You, and that's not what this is, but I do intend to listen more closely in church and read my Bible more often. Your word is so rich and filled with answers I haven't exactly paid attention to in the past. I want to live a life that is pleasing to You, Lord. Amen.

Kathryn knew her prayer was awkward, but she also knew the Lord understood. She was taking baby steps in her walk with the Lord, and there were times she staggered.

The next day was filled with meal preparation, washing sheets, vacuuming the foyer, dusting, and getting the downstairs room ready for Aunt Celia. One of the boarders was happy to move upstairs, since he'd been a regular customer at the City House for years. He even helped them move the furniture around to make it easier to maneuver the wheelchair.

Finally, the day was over, the last dish from dinner put away, and all the boarders in their rooms—except Stan. He remained behind, obviously waiting for Kathryn.

"I have to go back to Nashville before Christmas," he said without pause.

Okay, so what else was new? She just stared at him.

"I did promise to be here to help with your aunt."

"Yes, I know, but I can deal with it." Just like she'd had to deal with her father's empty promises throughout her childhood.

He glanced down and stared at his shoes as silence fell between them. Kathryn figured there was nothing left to say, so she turned to go to her room.

"No, wait," he said quickly.

She spun around. "What?"

"Kathryn, I'm really sorry. I'll be here for a little

while, though, so I can make sure all the heavy lifting is done before I go."

"You don't have to," she said.

"You're right, I don't. But I want to."

She sighed. "Okay, whatever."

This time, he let her go. She walked slowly up the stairs, but he didn't try to stop her. She'd been at Miss Celia's for a year, yet she still couldn't figure out what was going on with Stan.

As hard as it was to walk away, it was even harder to kneel beside her bed. She lowered her face into her hands and let the frustrations take over. One thing Kathryn didn't do, though, was cry. She'd learned long ago that crying didn't do her any good. Besides, if someone saw her red-eyed and tear-streaked, they would feel sorry for her, and she hated pity.

Finally, she stammered over another prayer, this one expressing her disappointment but willingness to continue to try to walk in the path He had in mind for her—obviously without Stan.

"I've ordered a car to take her home," Stan said first thing the next morning.

"I was going to call a cab."

"Humor me. This is my way of paying her back for being so good to me."

189

"Okay," she said as numbness flooded her. "What time?"

He glanced at his watch. "I called when I got up this morning, and the nurse said the doctor would probably release her around ten."

"Fine."

Stan looked at her in silence for several seconds and then turned and walked away. She hated that tugging sensation at her chest as he disappeared from her life once again.

The excited murmurs from the guests showed how much Aunt Celia was loved. A couple of the men hung streamers, and one of the women had made a "WELCOME HOME, MISS CELIA" banner on her laptop computer and portable printer. Those who could arrange it took the day off from business meetings and school so they could greet Aunt Celia when she arrived. Kathryn pretended to be in a festive mood right along with the rest of them.

"Mind if I go to the rehab center with you?" Stan asked.

"Suit yourself." She didn't look him in the eye as they headed outside.

When they arrived at the rehab center, Aunt Celia was in her last therapy session. All the nursing assistants and technicians hugged her, saying to call and let them know how she was doing. True to form, Aunt Celia invited them to the City House for dinner one night soon, saying, "I'm sure my niece wouldn't mind making something fabulous. She's a trained chef, ya know."

The pride in her voice boosted Kathryn's mood. It was nice having someone recognize her talent rather than hearing the complaints about the "fancy cooking."

"Ready to hit the road?" Stan asked as he gripped the wheelchair handles and wheeled her out to the waiting car.

"You got that right. I'm ready to bust outta this joint."

The boardinghouse was suspiciously still as they pulled up in front. "It's good to be home," Aunt Celia said softly. "I hardly got any rest at the hospital."

Those words were barely out of her mouth when the door flung open and all twelve guests piled out onto the front porch. "Surprise!" they yelled. "Welcome home, Miss Celia!"

She covered her mouth with her hands as tears streamed down her cheeks. This was the first time Kathryn had ever seen her aunt cry, and if she hadn't looked away, she would be sobbing right along with her.

Chapter 8

Stan glanced at Kathryn and winked. She looked away and tried to blend in with the others.

Kathryn noticed Aunt Celia's smile beginning to fade after an hour of everyone talking at the same time. "Why don't we take you to your room for a while?" she whispered. "You look like you could use the rest."

Aunt Celia nodded gratefully. "You're right. I'm exhausted."

"Make way for Miss Celia," Gus said as he grabbed the wheelchair handles and pushed toward her room. He got to the door then nodded to Kathryn. "Why don't you take over from here? I don't want to force my way into a lady's room."

Aunt Celia appeared to bite back a smile, but she

didn't say a word as Kathryn took over. Once the bedroom door was shut, with Kathryn and Aunt Celia inside, they looked at each other and laughed.

"This is all so sweet, but I was hoping to get a little shut-eye before having to face the crowd."

"I know," Kathryn said apologetically. "But you know how they are. They love you so much, they couldn't wait to see you."

"Wake me in time to help out with dinner," Aunt Celia said.

"You're kidding, right?"

"No, I'm not kidding. I'm back now, and I plan to do the work I've been doing practically all my life."

"If you insist," Kathryn said, knowing there was no point in arguing.

"What's going on between you and Stan?"

Kathryn did a double take. "What do you mean?"

"I've seen the way you two have been avoiding each other. Something's up."

"Nothing's up. He told me he was going back to Nashville in a few days. I think his time here has come to an end."

"Oh, I see."

Kathryn helped Aunt Celia to her bed; then she leaned over and planted a kiss on her cheek. "Get some rest. I'll be back in a few hours."

"Don't forget."

"Sleep tight." Kathryn shut the door behind her, looking down at the floor. She'd taken two steps without looking up when she was stopped by a shadow that suddenly appeared in the hallway. She blinked as she glanced toward the movement.

"Is she all squared away?" Stan asked. He took up half the hallway with his presence.

With a nod, Kathryn replied, "She wants me to wake her to help with dinner." She hoped he couldn't hear her heart pounding.

"That woman is a human dynamo. Nothing stops her, does it?"

"Never has," Kathryn said as she tried to edge around him. He paused then stepped to the side to let her pass.

As she brushed past him, she held her breath. His nearness unnerved her.

Once she was out of his sight, Kathryn leaned against the wall. The instant she'd seen Stan standing in the hall looking at her, her knees had weakened, and she felt that odd sensation in the pit of her stomach. Now she barely had the strength to stand. Even imagining him in prison and remembering how he'd deserted her time after time didn't erase her desire to be with him. Avoiding him was the only way to get past that.

Dinner was a major production, since she wanted Aunt Celia to be proud of the fact that she could handle being in charge of the kitchen. An hour before dinner was to be served, Kathryn went to get her aunt.

"Hello, dear." Aunt Celia was sitting up in her bed and brushing her hair when Kathryn entered the room.

"You're awake."

"I got plenty of rest. I'm so happy to be here, I almost can't be still."

"I'm happy to have you back," Kathryn replied. "And so is everyone else."

They'd barely made it to the kitchen when Aunt Celia took control. "Put me to work."

Kathryn was amazed at how quickly her aunt had adjusted, and she said so. "I've been doing this practically all my life," Aunt Celia reminded her. "It's in my blood."

"You're amazing," Kathryn said.

Aunt Celia looked at her with a contemplative expression. "*God* is amazing. I'm letting Him do His work through me."

"Yes, God is amazing, isn't He?"

"So, how's your Bible reading coming along, Kathryn?"

"Just fine. I've been paying close attention whenever someone mentions a verse," she said. "I'm using your mother's Bible."

"Good girl. That's what I was hoping you'd do." Aunt Celia turned toward Bonnie and held out a bowl. "Here's the sauce. Let me take a look at the cake you're working on."

She quickly took the helm in the kitchen, which Kathryn was more than happy to let her have.

A party atmosphere hung over dinner, and Aunt Celia clearly enjoyed herself. But after the last of the boarders went to their rooms, she sighed.

"That was exhausting," she said. "I don't remember it being like this."

Stan was by her side in a flash. "That's because you were used to being in the thick of things."

"I suppose," she said. She sniffed and wheeled her chair to the kitchen door. "I'd like to help clean up, but I'm not sure I can do much."

"Not tonight," Mona said. "You're supposed to relax on your first night home. We'll clean up."

"Are you sure?"

Kathryn noticed her aunt didn't argue, which meant she had to be bone-tired.

"Positive," Mona replied. "Stan, you help Kathryn

while I take Miss Celia back to her room."

Bonnie had to leave early, so Stan joined Kathryn in the kitchen. "Are you okay?" he asked.

"I'm fine."

"Okay, I won't push. I'm leaving in three days. I was sort of hoping. . ." He looked at her but didn't finish his sentence.

"Hoping what?"

Quickly turning his back to her, he said, "Nothing. Let's get this mess cleaned up, okay?"

By the time Mona returned from helping Aunt Celia, they'd washed all the dishes and most of the pots and pans. Mona nudged Stan out of the way and told him that he could leave now.

After he was gone, she turned to Kathryn. "Everything will work out like it is supposed to."

"Yes, I know."

"God's plan is always greater than anything we can imagine."

Kathryn nodded as she lifted the scouring brush. They finished working side by side in silence.

For the next couple of days, Kathryn did her best to avoid Stan. But on the morning of his departure, he cornered her.

"I have something for you," he whispered.

"For me?"

"Yes," he said. He handed her a wrapped package. "Open it after I leave. I think it'll come in handy when you have questions."

Kathryn stood there and looked at the package she held in her hand. He reached out and gently touched her cheek. She quickly glanced up at him.

"Kathryn," he said softly, "you're a very good woman. I wish things could be different between us."

She couldn't speak. His touch was soft yet full of meaning—just like his words.

Chapter 9

For a moment, she thought he might try to kiss her. But he didn't. Instead, his lips twitched into a slight smile, and he tweaked her nose.

"I'll see you again soon, I hope," he told her. "I really care about you, Kathryn."

All she could do now was watch him as he walked away from her—out of her life—probably forever. All hope she had of things being different was gone.

Before going to her own room, she decided to check up on her aunt. "Come chat for a few minutes," Aunt Celia said, patting the bed beside her.

Kathryn did as she was told.

"What's that?" Aunt Celia asked, pointing to the package.

"A gift from Stan," Kathryn replied.

"About Stan," Aunt Celia began. Kathryn stiffened but remained seated. "What he said about his past is 100 percent accurate. Before I allowed a former convict to stay in my boardinghouse, I had him checked out. He's a very good boy with a heart for Christ."

"You had him checked out?" Kathryn asked.

"Yes, of course I did. Running a boardinghouse is a huge responsibility. I can't risk the safety of my boarders by letting just anyone stay here."

Kathryn instantly felt ashamed of herself for doubting Stan. "I should have known."

"Good night, sweetheart. I'll say a prayer for you, and you do the same for me."

Later that night, with nervous fingers, Kathryn tore into the gift Stan had left. It was a Bible concordance, with a bright blue cover and her name inscribed in gold lettering. He could not have given her a more thoughtful gift.

She lost track of time as she looked up all the questions she'd had about forgiveness, mercy, and grace. The verses she read made God's message very clear—that only through Him can we have a full life. And it involved total trust in the Lord and not in man.

It was past midnight when she finally snuggled under the covers and nestled her head on the pillow.

Regrets filled her conscious thoughts. Maybe her relationship with Stan would have been different if she hadn't endured such a painful childhood. But then again, look at what he'd faced when being falsely accused. So what if her father hadn't been there when she'd needed him. It wasn't a good thing, but she'd survived. Now it was up to her to follow Christ and let go of her tortured past. She didn't have the right to transpose her hard feelings toward her father onto Stan, which was what she'd been doing since she'd learned about his past. She fell asleep wishing she'd allowed herself to follow God's lead with Stan.

The next several days were filled with a flurry of holiday arrangements. Most of the boarders planned to return to their homes.

Kathryn noticed her aunt's sincerity and warmth and how well other people responded to her. Aunt Celia was a living, breathing example of what Christ wanted his followers to be like.

The days passed quickly, and one by one the people left Miss Celia's City House. The place grew very quiet. There wasn't much work for Mona and Bonnie, so Aunt Celia alternated their days off.

"Do you ever worry about anything, Aunt Celia?" Kathryn asked one evening as they sat in front of the fireplace in the sitting room.

"Sometimes," Aunt Celia admitted. "But I know I'm being watched after, so I pray about it and let go."

"I'd like to be more like that," Kathryn said. "I worry way too much."

"You're right," Aunt Celia agreed. "You do worry too much. Just keep praying about it and let Him work in your heart."

In spite of the fact that they only had a couple of boarders in the house, Aunt Celia insisted on decorating for Christmas. She did what she could by herself and told Kathryn where to put lights and holly.

"I think that wreath will look much better over there," she said, pointing to the door.

Suddenly, as if on command, the door opened. Aunt Celia turned to Kathryn with a curious glance then turned back to the door.

In walked Stan, grinning and bearing a stack of gifts that towered above his head. He peeked around his armload of packages. "Merry Christmas, Miss Celia. You didn't think I'd be able to stay away during this joyous time, did you?"

"Stan!" Aunt Celia squealed with delight. "Will you be here for Christmas?"

"No, I'm afraid not," he replied. "I'm leaving right

after the Christmas Eve services. I'm scheduled to fly back to Nashville late Christmas Eve."

"This is wonderful, Stan," Aunt Celia said. "At least we have you for part of the holiday." She turned to Kathryn and winked. "Right, Kathryn?"

"Uh, right." Kathryn looked around, trying to find something to focus on besides Stan's penetrating gaze.

"Put those boxes down and come help us decorate the rest of this house."

Stan did as he was told. By dinnertime, the entire house was decorated in greenery, tiny white lights, and red velvet bows. Kathryn loved all the external trappings of Christmas. And now that she'd been studying her Bible, she understood the depth of what the celebration was truly about.

Stan could tell something was different about Kathryn, so he kept his distance until he had a better idea of what was going on with her. When he'd gotten the call about doing the sermon in New York, he'd jumped on it—mainly because it gave him another opportunity to see Kathryn.

"We're due for a terrible storm," Aunt Celia said during dinner. "I've heard we may get up to two feet of snow."

"That's pretty rough," Stan said. "But as long as public transportation continues to run, we should be okay."

"I don't think that'll be a problem," Aunt Celia said.

"I'm fine as long as I can get to the prison on Christmas Eve." He placed his fork on his plate and looked down. "I'll have to leave for the airport directly from the jail if I want to make my flight."

"Do you have to leave right away?" Miss Celia asked.

He sighed and nodded. "You know how it is."

Kathryn was very quiet through dinner. When the last person finished dessert, she jumped up and started gathering dishes.

"Need some help?" he asked.

"Not really," Kathryn said as she disappeared behind the swinging door.

"Don't ask, Stan," Miss Celia said. "Just do it."

"I think she's avoiding me."

"Of course she is. That girl's been through a lot. You'll have to prove yourself to her."

"I shouldn't have to prove myself to anyone," he argued.

Miss Celia's shook her head and gestured for him to follow her. "We need to talk," she told him.

Once they were sure no one was behind them, Miss Celia instructed him to close the door to the sitting room. "Apparently, there are some things you don't understand about my niece."

He shrugged. "Maybe you're right, but I do know she's determined to be a successful chef."

"My brother really did a number on her. He not only spent time in prison, he lied to her constantly."

"He lied? About what?"

"You name it, he lied about it. He kept promising to come back for her and her mother. He came back a couple of times, but he only stuck around until he had enough money to leave again."

"She told me about her father going to jail. That's hard on a kid. I see it all the time. At least she had her mother."

Miss Celia snickered. "What did she tell you about her mother?"

"Kathryn said she's an actress in local theater."

"Dinner theater in Boise, Idaho," Miss Celia said with disdain. "That's not exactly the most family-friendly profession a mother can have. She was gone all the time and often left Kathryn home alone until the wee hours of the night. When Kathryn got up, her mother was always sound asleep. They were like two ships passing in the night."

"That's even worse than I realized." No wonder she

acted so distant each time he announced he was leaving.

Miss Celia sighed. "I tried to make things better for her when I had her here during the summers. I taught her how to cook because that mother of hers can't even boil an egg."

"She did mention something about having to cook her own meals, but she doesn't seem to have minded."

"You're right," Miss Celia agreed. "She's always been a natural in the kitchen. Unfortunately, she doesn't see the value in a simple, home-cooked meal. Her mother was pretentious, and she loved ordering gourmet foods, which was what Kathryn was brought up eating when she was at home. When she came here, she always doctored up everything I cooked for her."

"There's nothing wrong with being a gourmet chef," Stan said in Kathryn's defense.

"That's true. But there are times when I wish Kathryn would relax a little and not be so intense about her life. She wants to force things, when she needs to be quiet and pay attention to what the Lord wants for her."

"I think she's heading in that direction," Stan said.

"Well, she has been reading her Bible—and that concordance you gave her."

"I need to talk to her."

"You're a good boy, Stan," Miss Celia said. Was that

a guilty glimmer in her eye?

"Thanks," he said. "I think."

She tilted her head back and let out a deep chuckle. "You think I'm up to something, don't you?"

"Miss Celia," he replied, "now that you bring it up, I *know* you're up to something."

"Smart boy."

Kathryn was wiping her hands on a towel right when Stan wheeled Miss Celia's chair into the kitchen. Miss Celia didn't give him a chance to say a word.

"Why don't the two of you go string some popcorn in the front room? I want to spend a little time alone in the kitchen."

Stan watched as Kathryn's eyes quickly developed a look of fear and helplessness. He wanted to give her an out, but he wasn't sure how to do it with Miss Celia sitting there glaring at them, almost as if daring either of them to argue.

Chapter 10

Kathryn finally nodded. "Okay, but I need to go to bed soon. I haven't finished my shopping, so I'm getting up early to get my work done."

"Don't worry about that, sweetie. There's not much to do around here when we only have a few guests."

Kathryn didn't utter another word as she quickly dropped the towel and headed toward the sitting room, where Miss Celia had instructed them to put the bowls of popcorn earlier. Stan was right behind her, unsure of what they'd talk about. He didn't want to tell her what he'd just discussed with her aunt, since he hadn't had time to digest all the information yet.

"Think we'll have a white Christmas?" Kathryn asked, breaking the silence between them.

"I hope so."

He studied her face as she picked up a kernel of corn and stabbed it with the needle. He wondered what she was thinking.

They strung popcorn in silence, with occasional comments about the weather for nearly an hour.

"I think this is enough," she finally said as she stood and carefully placed the strung popcorn in the bowl. "I'll ask Aunt Celia where she wants this hung and then I think I'll go to bed."

Stan stood and followed her to her aunt's room, where she rapped on the door. Miss Celia had somehow managed to get herself into bed. She was propped up reading the Bible.

"Whatcha reading, Miss Celia?" Stan asked.

"Isaiah," she replied. "Chapter fifty-three is mighty powerful."

"That it is," Stan agreed.

"Aunt Celia, what would you like us to do with this?" Kathryn asked, holding up the bowl of strung popcorn.

"Just put that in some plastic bags in the kitchen," she instructed Kathryn. "We can hang that tomorrow."

❧

Kathryn was too aware of Stan's presence as they headed upstairs to their rooms. When she got to the landing, she turned to face him.

"Thanks for all your help, Stan."

"My pleasure," he said, standing there looking down at her, his hands shoved into his pockets. He didn't look like he was eager to go anywhere.

Thoughts and emotions swirled inside her. Her resolve to accept Stan at face value hadn't been tested, and she wasn't sure what to do next.

"Do you have a big Christmas planned with your family?" Kathryn asked.

"No, not really. We generally just have a small get-together, and we exchange gifts. Most of the time, we go to Christmas Eve service together the night before, but things are a little different this year, with my ministry being what it is." His words were slow and slightly stilted, showing his discomfort.

"I bet it's hard on you."

"I'm fine with it. I don't get too hung up on expectations."

"Good night, Stan," Kathryn said, as she reluctantly turned her back and slipped into her room.

As the door closed behind her, she heard him say, "Good night, sweet Kathryn."

She crossed the room, sat on the edge of her bed, lifted her Bible, and turned to the same chapter her aunt had been reading. As she got ready for bed, she pondered the message and felt the impact from the words. With all of the Christmas decorations and festivities around her, Kathryn knew how easy it was to get lost in the worldly view of the season. She shut her eyes and began to pray.

Lord, you have revealed yourself to me in a way I never understood until now. All my life, I have tried to figure everything out on my own. But now, my eyes have been opened, thanks to Aunt Celia and. . .Stan. You have put me in the position of having to be still and listen, and for that, I thank you. Please continue to make my way clear and keep me close to you, Lord. Amen.

When Kathryn awoke the next morning, she shivered. There was a slight break between the curtain panels, revealing the light dusting of snow that had accumulated on the pane and the pile of white fluff on the sill. Pulling her blanket to her chin, she sat up slightly to see if the snow was still falling.

"Whoa!" she said as she realized it was not only snowing, it was coming down fast.

She leaned over, grabbed her robe off the footboard,

and then slipped her arms into it while remaining under the covers. A deep chill hung in the air, making her skin tingle as she quickly stuck out her feet and slid them into her big, fuzzy slippers. This was one of those mornings it was hard to get out of bed, but she had things to do.

Kathryn managed to shower and dress in record time, since she didn't want to be late getting a warm breakfast on the table. Aunt Celia was in the kitchen, waiting for her.

"G'morning, sweetie," Aunt Celia said. "The coffee will be ready in a few minutes."

The aroma of Aunt Celia's blueberry muffins—Kathryn's favorite—hung in the air. The coffeepot popped and sputtered as it brewed. Kathryn found comfort in the familiar morning sounds and smells.

"How did you manage to do all this?" Kathryn asked. "Did Mona come in?"

"No, dear, I did it by myself. But it wasn't too hard, since the girls put everything within my reach."

Kathryn remembered that Mona had suggested they do this, knowing Aunt Celia thrived on being independent. She said it would make Miss Celia crazy if she couldn't do a few things for herself.

"Have you looked outside?" Kathryn asked as she

sat down across from her aunt to wait for the coffee.

"I sure have. It's lovely, isn't it?"

"Yes," Kathryn agreed. "And very cold. I wonder if Stan will be able to get around in all this."

"I was wondering the same thing." Aunt Celia frowned. "When I turned on the news this morning, the weather forecaster said there was some concern about having to shut down the airport. This is only the beginning of the storm."

Kathryn stiffened. "What'll he do?"

Aunt Celia shook her head. "Nothing he can do but stick around here a few more days."

"Won't that mess up his plans?"

"Of course it will, but it's out of his hands. He'll be fine."

"Wow!" said a male voice from the kitchen door.

Both Kathryn and Aunt Celia turned around as Stan took a step toward them. Kathryn's pulse quickened.

"Have you looked outside?" he asked.

"Of course we have," Aunt Celia replied. "Help yourself to some coffee."

"Looks like we'll have our white Christmas after all," he said. "I need to leave for the jail early. It might take a little longer to get there."

Aunt Celia palmed the wheels of her chair, turning

it around. "I need to go to my room for a little while. Kathryn, would you mind cooking some sausage links?"

"Sure, Aunt Celia. I'll be glad to fix some."

After she was gone, Stan put his coffee mug down on the table and leaned toward Kathryn. "You do realize you're the daughter your aunt never had, don't you?"

Kathryn nodded. "She's always been very good to me. We're closer than most mothers and daughters."

"You're very fortunate, you know."

"Yes."

"Your aunt's not the only one who loves being around you," he said before picking up his mug again and taking a sip. "I must admit, I hope the airport is closed. It'll give me an opportunity to spend one of the most revered days of the year with you and your aunt. Being with you makes me very happy, Kathryn."

Chapter 11

Kathryn's cheeks grew hot. "Uh. . ." She stood up and made her way over to the counter beside the stove. "I really need to start the sausage, Stan."

"Let me help," he said.

"You really don't have to."

"Would you like for me to leave you alone?" he asked softly.

Confusion flooded Kathryn. She wanted him there, next to her, and she wanted him to leave so she could think straight. And she needed to be alone to pray for guidance.

"It would probably be best if you did," she replied.

He didn't say a word, so all she heard was the swinging door as it flipped open and swished back and forth until it stilled. Now that she was alone in the kitchen, she could think logically, without the intrusion of his presence. When she exhaled, she felt as if the burdens of her past had lifted from her shoulders, allowing her to follow His lead as she prayed for direction.

Kathryn had the sausage ready in minutes. She carried a platter of sausage and a basket of Aunt Celia's muffins into the breakfast area right outside the kitchen. To her surprise, the only person there was Aunt Celia.

"Stan had to leave," Aunt Celia explained. "The weather isn't going to improve, so I told him to go ahead to the prison."

Kathryn nodded as she poured two cups of coffee. "That's probably for the best." Disappointment muddied her thoughts.

Aunt Celia glared at her, lips pursed and jaws tight for several seconds before shaking her head. "I promised myself I'd stay out of this, but I'm afraid it's too much for me. Kathryn, why are you running away from Stan?"

"I'm not running."

"Maybe not physically, but you are emotionally. It's painful for me to watch you turn your back on something so special."

"You have to understand, Aunt Celia. It's been very hard for me to deal with my feelings about him."

Her voice trailed off as Aunt Celia nodded. "I understand, sweetheart, but Stan is nothing like your father."

Kathryn looked down at her feet and then back up at her aunt. "Yes, I know."

"Are you worried he's not telling the truth about his past?"

"At first I was, but not anymore," Kathryn admitted. "But there is one thing about him that baffles me."

"That he's not angry?" Aunt Celia said.

Kathryn nodded. "Most people would be fighting the system that unjustly accused them—but not Stan. He actually joined the ones who wrongly pointed their finger at him."

Aunt Celia smiled as she broke open a muffin and slathered it with softened butter. "His faith has provided him with the understanding that this is an unjust world we live in. Our rewards don't always come immediately. We seek eternal salvation through our faith in Christ, who never lets us down."

Kathryn hung her head as humility washed over her. "I'm so sorry, Aunt Celia," Kathryn said, her voice coming out in a squeak.

"Don't beat yourself up over this, dear. The Lord understands. After what you went through as a child, it would be difficult to trust anyone, especially a man."

"What can I do?" Kathryn asked.

"I know you care about Stan. I can see it in your eyes when you look at him."

"Am I that obvious?"

"Afraid so," Aunt Celia replied. "But if it's any consolation, he feels the same about you."

"You know it'll be difficult for me to have any kind of relationship with Stan, since he'll be in Tennessee and I'll be in Florida." She paused and then added, "After you fully recover, that is."

"Why don't you just relax and let the Lord take over?" Aunt Celia suggested. "In the meantime, enjoy your breakfast."

Just then, the phone rang, and Kathryn jumped. Fully expecting the call to be for Aunt Celia, she answered with a crisp, "Hello." It was the head chef at the Don Cesar.

"Kathryn, we have an unexpected opening in the kitchen. How soon can you be here?"

She glanced at Aunt Celia, who sat there picking at a muffin. Their conversation flashed through her mind, instantly letting her know what she had to do. "I'm sorry, but something has come up. I'm afraid you'll need to find someone else."

He gasped. "Are you certain of this? Working here is the opportunity of a lifetime."

"Yes, I know. But I really can't." She felt no remorse whatsoever.

She hung up the phone as her chest constricted. In one quick moment, she'd erased the future she'd always thought she wanted. Aunt Celia looked at her but didn't say a word.

"That was the chef at the Don Cesar."

"I'm very sorry, Kathryn dear. There will be something else, although I'm sure you don't see it now."

"Don't you understand, Aunt Celia? I'm now free to follow the Lord's will."

❦

Stan was so happy he could hardly contain himself. As soon as he'd walked in the front door of the prison, the head warden had cornered him.

"Congrats, Reverend. We had an unexpected job opening. You're now officially on staff. That is, if you still want the job."

"Are you kidding?" Stan asked.

"Nope, I'm serious as a judge. Your boys in the group you're preachin' to said they wanted you for the job, and the higher-ups actually listened." He chuckled and smacked his mouth. "Imagine that."

"Hey, thanks, pal. This is great news."

Miss Celia would be almost as happy as he was. She'd encouraged him to find a way to stay in New York since the need was so great. Telling her would be fun.

Then there was Kathryn. Stan blew out a long sigh as he thought about how much she'd come to mean to him. He didn't miss the irony of how he could now call New York his home while she'd be leaving for Florida when Miss Celia recovered.

Too bad, though. New York City agreed with her. He hadn't missed how she seemed to come alive as they went from the butcher to the green grocer. He wondered if she'd be happy in Florida.

Outside, Stan pulled his jacket tighter around him and leaned into the wind. The snow blew at a nearly forty-five-degree angle. The weather might be dreadful, but today it didn't bother him.

He stuck up his hand and captured the attention of one of the few cabs left on the street. Normally, he took the trains and walked, but these were extenuating circumstances, what with the weather and his eagerness to tell Miss Celia the good news.

The cab driver was chatty, talking about how he'd been hoping for a white Christmas. "I never expected this, though. I hope my kids aren't bouncing off the walls when I get home."

"Any idea how far behind schedule the flights are running at the airport?" Stan asked.

The cab driver lifted an eyebrow. "You're kidding, right? All flights today and tomorrow have been canceled."

An odd sort of peacefulness came over Stan as they inched toward Soho. He couldn't think of anything more enchanting than being snowbound with Kathryn and Miss Celia.

"Merry Christmas," Stan said, as the cab pulled to a stop in front of Miss Celia's City House.

After paying the driver, he carefully walked up the sidewalk to the steps. On the front door hung a green wreath with a large, red velvet bow. He had to use his shoulder to push the door open. He'd stayed here long enough to know it stuck with weather changes.

Miss Celia was sitting in the front room working on a jigsaw puzzle. "You alone?" he asked.

She glanced up, grinned, and nodded. "For now, anyway. Kathryn went up to nap. She's been working awfully hard lately, and I'm afraid she's not sleeping well at night. That girl has a lot on her mind."

"I'm sure she does."

Miss Celia looked up from her puzzle. "You look like you're ready to burst. What's going on?"

"You always could see right through me, Miss Celia." He paused a moment as she continued staring at him, waiting. "I've been offered a job on staff at the prison."

Miss Celia dropped the puzzle piece, and sincere joy lit up her face.

"I'm so happy for you, Stan."

"I hope you haven't already rented out my room."

Suddenly, her joyous expression turned cloudy. "I'm not sure yet."

"Hey, don't worry about it. I'm sure the Lord will provide something if you've got my room rented to someone else."

"It's not that," she said slowly. "It's just—"

Kathryn suddenly appeared. "Oh, hi, Stan," she said before turning to her aunt. "Do you think I should make cheesecake for dessert?"

"That would be wonderful," Miss Celia replied. "Won't it, Stan?"

"Absolutely, yes."

He saw the slight hint of a blush in her cheeks as she nodded. "Okay, then, we're having leg of lamb, asparagus tips, and cheesecake for dessert."

"I told her to pull out all the stops for dinner tonight," Miss Celia explained. "She must be getting tired of holding back."

"Actually, I've enjoyed cooking for your boarders, Aunt Celia," Kathryn said as she lingered in the doorway, "after I got used to it. I'd better get back to work."

Miss Celia cleared her throat. "Why don't you make yourself useful in the kitchen, Stan? I'm sure Kathryn could use a helping hand."

"Yes, of course." He pulled himself away from the table and left the room.

❧

Kathryn was fully aware of what her aunt was up to, but now she didn't mind. Aunt Celia was a hopeless romantic.

"Sorry about my aunt," Kathryn said once she and Stan were alone in the kitchen. "She's not exactly the most subtle person in the world."

"Subtlety is overrated," he replied. "I've got some good news."

"Good news?" she said, spinning around to face him. "What?"

"I've been offered a permanent position at the prison."

"Oh, Stan, that's wonderful." He seemed surprised by her enthusiastic response.

"There's only one problem, though."

"What's that?"

"You won't be here."

Kathryn felt her chest constrict and a lump form in her throat. "You never know what the Lord will do next." She'd tell him her news later.

"What can I do to help?" he asked.

"Help?"

"Yes. Help with dinner."

"Oh. Uh, no, that's okay. I have everything under control."

"Then I'll go hang out with your aunt until you call for us."

Every few minutes, Kathryn glanced outside to observe the heavy snowfall. The entire backyard was buried under a thick quilt of snow. No one with an ounce of good sense would be out there in this mess. She was glad she'd ordered extra food that had been delivered when the roads were still passable.

Just as she put the finishing touches on the lamb, the kitchen door swung open. She half expected it to be Stan, but it wasn't. It was Aunt Celia, taking tentative steps, using her walker. Kathryn quickly dropped what she was doing and rushed to her aunt's side.

"Why don't you wait a few more days before attempting this?" she asked.

"I don't believe in waiting for anything," Aunt Celia replied. She dropped into the nearest chair and exclaimed, "Whew! Who knew walking a few steps could be so exhausting?"

Kathryn wished her aunt would be more careful, since not even an ambulance would be able to navigate the streets of New York during such a heavy snowstorm. "Stay right there. I'll get Stan and see if he wants to have dinner in here."

"That would be cozy," Aunt Celia agreed. "There's no point in hauling all the food to the dining room for just the three of us. There are some things I need to discuss with you and Stan, anyway. I hope you don't mind."

Chapter 12

S tan had just finished saying the blessing when Aunt Celia piped up. "I've had a very generous offer on this place."

Kathryn froze, her fork suspended by the tips of her fingers in midair. "Offer? What kind of offer?"

"With the price of property skyrocketing in Soho, this place is worth a fortune. Plus, I'm afraid this boardinghouse is the last of a dying industry."

Stan frowned. "But where will you go?"

She flashed a smile toward Stan, then reached out and placed her hand on Kathryn's arm. "As I'm sure you're aware, I'm not getting any younger. My accident opened my eyes to the fact that it's time for me to look into other. . .living arrangements."

"Like what?" Kathryn said.

"My church sponsors a retirement center. The place stays pretty full, but there's an opening coming up. I'd like to move there, and the executive director said she'd hold it for me."

"I'm familiar with the place," Stan said. "It's nice."

"But you can't move to a retirement home, Aunt Celia. What about all your boarders?"

Aunt Celia shrugged. "I've stayed open for them as long as I can. I'm sure they'll find someplace just as nice."

"But what about all these great meals? There's nothing else like the food here—at least not in the city."

Kathryn caught what appeared to be a warning glance from Stan, but Aunt Celia smiled, looking back and forth between them. "Maybe I can talk someone into opening a restaurant and using my recipes. Besides, things change all the time. I can only do so much."

"I'm sure you've prayed about this, Miss Celia," Stan said. "I'll support whatever you decide to do."

"Yes, I know you will," she replied. "I was hoping I'd get a blessing from both of you." She tilted her head forward as she looked at Kathryn.

"Yes, of course," Kathryn said quickly. "I just hope you don't regret it." Her appetite quickly vanished.

"I'm ready for your fabulous cheesecake," Stan said a little too cheerfully.

"Me, too," Aunt Celia said.

Kathryn stood quickly, nearly knocking over her chair. She couldn't help but notice the glance exchanged between Aunt Celia and Stan as she scurried toward the counter.

Both of them made all the right appreciative sounds as they ate dessert. Stan had seconds, and Aunt Celia said she wished she could, too, but that she wasn't getting enough exercise to work off the calories. Finally, she asked for help to her room so she could go to bed early.

"Why don't you two have a little Bible study?" Aunt Celia said. "Take advantage of the blessings of this weather and spend it in prayer?"

"Sounds like a wonderful idea," Stan said as he steadied her on her walker. "But first, I want to make sure you're safe and warm in your bed. I'll be right back to help with the dishes, Kathryn."

"You're such a lovely boy," Kathryn heard her aunt say as they left the kitchen. "Any girl would be blessed to have you."

Kathryn's shoulders sagged as she realized how right her aunt was. Stan was a real keeper. He'd been through the most trying of times—much worse than anything she'd had to face—yet he never lost his faith in God. The saddest part of her realization was that she'd blown any chance she had with him by being so stubborn in the beginning.

Kathryn slowly bowed her head and whispered a prayer for forgiveness. "Lord, I've been selfish. Please show me what You want for me and make me pay attention." As she said the short, simple prayer aloud, she heard a shuffling behind her.

"I think you know what He wants for you," Stan said softly. "Both of us have been fighting it, but we can't any longer."

Kathryn turned around and faced him, trying hard to will her cheeks not to turn pink. But she couldn't stop them. They heated up just like they always did when she was alone with Stan.

"I didn't want to fall in love with you, Kathryn. You have all these big plans to make your way in the culinary world."

"What about you?" she asked. "You've got mighty big plans of your own."

"Yes, but until now, I never thought my dreams would come true. I had to wait for the Lord's timing to get this great offer. The only thing that bothers me is that you'll be down in sunny Florida."

"I almost forgot to tell you."

"Tell me what?"

"I got a call from the chef at the Don Cesar in Florida. He wanted me to come down there immediately, but I told him I was no longer interested."

Stan took a step closer. He tentatively reached out and touched her cheek. "What does this mean?"

"It means I'd like to stick around New York for a while."

"There must be dozens of places in the city that would love to hire you," Stan said, his grin widening.

"That's not what I had in mind. In fact, I might even open my own restaurant. Aunt Celia was throwing enough hints."

"Excellent idea," he said.

She twisted her mouth as she thought some more. "Of course, I have to find a place to live, and I just gave up my apartment in Midtown."

"Maybe we can go apartment hunting together," he said.

Kathryn nodded. "Yeah, and bounce ideas off each other."

"We can visit each other and talk about our new jobs. Maybe you can cook for me, and I can help you do a few things around your place."

She swallowed and nodded. "Great idea."

He glanced down at his feet and then looked back at her. "Who am I trying to kid? I don't want to visit you."

"You don't?"

"No, I don't. What I really want is. . ."

Kathryn watched him expectantly as his expression changed. "What do you really want?"

"What I really want is. . .Kathryn, I love you. I want you to be my wife. . .then we can get an apartment together."

A bolt of joy flashed through her. As soon as she realized her chin had dropped, she clamped her mouth shut.

"Well?" he said. "I guess I did spring that on you without warning. Will you marry me?"

Kathryn was overcome by a fit of nervous giggles. "Yes, Stan, I'll marry you."

He blew out a sigh of relief. "For a moment there, I was afraid you'd say no, that you didn't want to be tied down."

"For a man of faith, that doesn't sound right," she said.

"I'm only human." He pulled her into his arms and dropped a kiss onto her forehead. "Who would've thought that such a wonderful thing would come of being snowbound for Christmas?"

"It just goes to show how prayer works."

Epilogue

H ow's it going?" Stan asked as he entered the kitchen of the tiny restaurant and catering service Kathryn had opened three months after their wedding. Their first Christmas as a married couple was coming up fast, and Stan had hoped they'd have some quiet time together. . .but from the looks of things, that wouldn't happen for a while.

"I'm swimming in sugar," she replied.

Stan chuckled. "I always wondered what made you so sweet. Now I know."

She cast a coquettish glance at him and giggled. "You know what I mean. I have so many orders for cheesecakes, macaroons, and crème brulees, I'm not sure Bonnie and I can handle it."

"Sure you can, sweetheart," Stan said as he reached

out and grabbed one of the macaroons she'd placed on a platter to cool. "I'm just glad you came to your senses and hired someone who could keep up with you in the kitchen."

"Have you told Aunt Celia the news?" Kathryn asked.

"No, I thought you might want to be with me when I do."

"She'll be happy for us."

"And she'll be even happier when she finds out that if this baby is a girl, we're naming her Celia Rose, after her and your mother."

Stan came up behind her and and gently patted her slightly protruding abdomen, letting the warmth of their love and God's blessings envelop them.

CHEF KATHRYN'S NEW YORK CHEESECAKE

Crust

    1 c. graham cracker crumbs
    ¼ c. granulated sugar
    ¼ c. melted butter
    ¼ t. vanilla extract

Combine graham cracker crumbs, sugar, and vanilla. Mix well. Pat into the bottom of a 9-inch buttered springform pan. Trim. Bake at 400°F for five minutes to set. Cool.

Filling

    2 lbs. cream cheese
    1⅓ c. sugar
    4 eggs
    2 T. all-purpose flour
    2 t. grated lemon zest
    ¼ c. heavy cream

In a mixer, combine cream cheese and sugar until blended. Add eggs and blend until smooth. Mix in flour, lemon zest, and cream. Pour into crust-lined pan. Bake in a preheated 400°F oven for ten minutes; reduce temperature to 300ºF and continue baking 35 minutes longer. Let cool. Chill before serving. To serve, remove pan sides and cut into wedges. Garnish with fresh fruit.

Debby Mayne has been a freelance writer for as long as she can remember, starting with short slice-of-life stories in small newspapers, then moving on to parenting articles for regional publications and fiction stories for women and girls. She has been involved in all aspects of publishing from the creative side, to editing a national health publication, to freelance proofreading for several book publishers. Her belief that all blessings come from the Lord has given her great comfort during trying times and gratitude for when she is rewarded for her efforts. She lives on the west coast of Florida with her husband and two daughters.

A Letter to Our Readers

Dear Readers:

In order that we might better contribute to your reading enjoyment, we would appreciate your taking a few minutes to respond to the following questions. When completed, please return to the following: Fiction Editor, Barbour Publishing, Inc., P.O. Box 719, Uhrichsville, OH 44683.

1. Did you enjoy reading *Snowbound for Christmas*?
   ❑ Very much—I would like to see more books like this.
   ❑ Moderately—I would have enjoyed it more if _____
   _____
   _____

2. What influenced your decision to purchase this book?
   (Check those that apply.)
   ❑ Cover   ❑ Back cover copy   ❑ Title   ❑ Price
   ❑ Friends   ❑ Publicity   ❑ Other

3. Which story was your favorite?
   ❑ *Let It Snow*   ❑ *Christmas in the City*

4. Please check your age range:
   ❑ Under 18   ❑ 18–24   ❑ 25–34
   ❑ 35–45   ❑ 46–55   ❑ Over 55

5. How many hours per week do you read? _____

Name _____

Occupation _____

Address _____

City_____ State_____ Zip_____

E-mail_____

If you enjoyed

SNOWBOUND
for
CHRISTMAS
then read:

A
PRAIRIE
CHRISTMAS

*A Pair of Novellas Celebrating
the Age-Old Season of Love*

One Wintry Night by Pamela Griffin
The Christmas Necklace by Maryn Langer

If you enjoyed

SNOWBOUND
for
CHRISTMAS

then read:

A Christmas
SLEIGH RIDE

A Double Delight of
Nostalgia in Two Romances

Colder Than Ice by Jill Stengl
Take Me Home by Tracey V. Bateman

HEARTSONG ♥ PRESENTS

Love Stories
Are Rated G!

That's for godly, gratifying, and of course, great! If you love a thrilling love story but don't appreciate the sordidness of some popular paperback romances, **Heartsong Presents** is for you. In fact, **Heartsong Presents** is the premiere inspirational romance book club featuring love stories where Christian faith is the primary ingredient in a marriage relationship.

Sign up today to receive your first set of four, never-before-published Christian romances. Send no money now; you will receive a bill with the first shipment. You may cancel at any time without obligation, and if you aren't completely satisfied with any selection, you may return the books for an immediate refund!

Imagine. . .four new romances every four weeks—two historical, two contemporary—with men and women like you who long to meet the one God has chosen as the love of their lives. . .all for the low price of $10.99 postpaid.

To join, simply complete the coupon below and mail to the address provided. **Heartsong Presents** romances are rated G for another reason: They'll arrive Godspeed!

YES! Sign me up for Heart♥ng!

NEW MEMBERSHIPS WILL BE SHIPPED IMMEDIATELY!
Send no money now. We'll bill you only $10.99 postpaid with your first shipment of four books. Or for faster action, call toll free 1-800-847-8270.

NAME _____

ADDRESS _____

CITY _____ STATE _____ ZIP _____

MAIL TO: HEARTSONG PRESENTS, P.O. Box 721, Uhrichsville, Ohio 44683
or visit www.heartsongpresents.com